WASTE PICKERS
in DHAKA

WASTE PICKERS
in DHAKA

Using the sustainable livelihoods approach

Key findings and field notes

Jonathan Rouse & Mansoor Ali

Water, Engineering and Development Centre
Loughborough University
2001

Water, Engineering and Development Centre,
Loughborough University,
Leicestershire, LE11 3TU, UK

© WEDC, Loughborough University, 2001

ISBN 13 Paperback: 978 0 90605 584 7
ISBN Ebook: 9781788533652
Book DOI: http://dx.doi.org/10.3362/9781788533652

A catalogue record for this book is available from the British Library.

A reference copy of this publication is also available online at:
http://www.lboro.ac.uk/wedc/publications/

Rouse, J. R. and Ali, S. M. (2001)
Waste Pickers in Dhaka:
Using the sustainable livelihoods approach - Key findings and field notes
WEDC, Loughborough University, UK.

WEDC (The Water, Engineering and Development Centre) at Loughborough University in the UK is one of the world's leading institutions concerned with education, training, research and consultancy for the planning, provision and management of physical infrastructure for development in low- and middleincome countries.

This edition is reprinted and distributed by Practical Action Publishing.
Since 1974, Practical Action Publishing has published and disseminated books and information in support of international development work throughout the world. Practical Action Publishing trades only in support of its parent charity objectives and any profits are covenanted back to Practical Action (Charity Reg. No. 247257, Group VAT Registration No. 880 9924 76).

All reasonable precautions have been taken by the WEDC, Loughborough University to verify the information contained in this publication. However, WEDC, Loughborough University does not necessarily endorse the technologies presented in this document. The published material is being distributed without warranty of any kind, either expressed or implied. The responsibility for the interpretation and use of the material lies with the reader. In no event shall the WEDC, Loughborough University be liable for damages as a result of their use.

Designed at WEDC
Photographs: Jonathan Rouse

About the authors

Jonathan Rouse is a Research Assistant at WEDC. He graduated with a B.Sc. in Physics from the University of Nottingham in 1997 and from the University of Sussex with an MA in Rural Development in 1999. He has since been working for WEDC in the field of sustainable livelihoods, and in India on a rural household energy project. He undertook the fieldwork for this research in Bangladesh in 2000.

Dr Mansoor Ali is a Project/Programme Manager at WEDC. As a specialist in solid waste management for low- and middle-income countries, he has researched and published extensively. Some of his current research projects include Waste and Livelihoods, Micro-enterprise Development, Appropriate Landfilling and Recycling.

Acknowledgements

The following people are gratefully acknowledged for the valuable contributions they made to this research.

Local collaborators
Hasnat Iftekhar Hossain   Fieldwork research assistant and translator.

Dr Babar Kabir, Dr Tanveer Ahsan and Shafiul Azam Ahmed of the Water and Sanitation Programme, Bangladesh for their advice and for enabling the author to use their office facilities whilst in Dhaka.

Others
Jenny Appleton   WEDC, UK
Rod Shaw   WEDC, UK
Sue Plummer   WEDC, UK
Martin Gillham   Mott MacDonald, Dhaka, Bangladesh.

Finally, thanks to all the waste pickers who contributed to this research.

Contents

Background   1

How this booklet is organised   2

Part I: Key findings   3

1.   Introduction   4
    1.1   Why research waste pickers in Dhaka?   4
    1.2   Who are waste pickers?   5
    1.3   The sustainable livelihoods approach   6

2.   Vulnerability context   9
    2.1   Shocks   9
    2.2   Trends   12
    2.3   Seasonality   12
    2.4   Vulnerability summary   19

3.   Asset profiles   21
    3.1   Human capital   21
    3.2   Social capital   24
    3.3   Natural capital   25
    3.4   Physical capital   30
    3.5   Financial Capital   32
    3.6   The asset pentagon   34

4.   Transforming structures and processes   36
    4.1   Structures   36
    4.2   Processes   37
    4.3   Access to infrastructure   38

5.   Livelihood strategies   39
    5.1   Livelihood 'straddling'   39
    5.2   Livelihood alternatives   40

6.   Livelihood outcomes   41
    6.1   Focus group ranking exercise   41

7.   The sustainable livelihoods approach as a tool   44
    7.1   How incisive?   44
    7.2   How relevant?   45
    7.3   How appropriate?   45
    7.4   How comprehensive?   45

8.	Conclusion	47
	8.1 The sustainable livelihoods approach	47
	8.2 The livelihoods of waste pickers	48
9.	Future research scope	50

Part II: Field notes | | 51

1.	Fieldwork methodology	52
	1.1 The researcher and local collaborators	52
	1.2 Time and duration of fieldwork	53
	1.3 Initial observations	53
	1.4 Research with individuals	53
	1.5 Research using focus groups	56
2.	Whose research and whose agenda?	58
	2.1 Listening to 'quiet voices'	58
	2.2 A note on gender	60
3.	Communication	61
	3.1 Language difficulties	61
	3.2 Articulation and group work	61
	3.3 Recognising different backgrounds and perspectives	64
	3.4 Invisible trends	67
	3.5 Ambiguity	68
4.	Other Issues	70
	4.1 Fear of authority and attitudes to field staff	70
	4.2 Crowds and attention	70
	4.3 Time	71
	4.4 Motivation behind answers	71
	4.5 Cross-checking and triangulation	72
	4.6 Generalisation	74
5.	Summary of findings	75
References		77
Bibliography		77
Internet sources		78
End notes		79

Acronyms

DFID Department for International Development

NGO Non-Governmental Organisation

SLA Sustainable Livelihoods Analysis

Boxes

Box 1: Training opportunities 22
Box 2: Monir and the effects of improved conservancy 29
Box 3: Dhaka *bustees* 31
Box 4: Girls in the Korail *bustee* 37
Box 5: Contrasting personalities: Saddam and Shahib Ali 58
Box 6: Who are we listening to? 59
Box 7: Understanding the question: making links 66
Box 8: Gentle suggestion technique 66
Box 9: Invisible trends 67
Box 10: An illustration of the pitfalls of ambiguity 69
Box 11: Triangulation: dealers' statements 72
Box 12: Discrepancies 73
Box 13: Field worker questions 76

Figures

Figure 1.   Mirpur hostel seasonal chart   16
Figure 2.   Korail *bustee* seasonal chart   17
Figure 3.   Asset pentagon   34
Figure 4.   Pictures used in the Korail seasonal chart   63
Figure 5.   Cards used in the ranking exercise   65

Photographs

Photograph 1.   Pickers carrying waste at Matuail landfill   5
Photograph 2.   Pickers around the diggers at Matuail landfill   10
Photograph 3.   Mirpur group seasonal chart   15
Photograph 4.   Raju and Jushim in the Begum Bari *bustee*   31
Photograph 5.   Mirpur boys arranging ranking cards   40
Photograph 6.   Field work in Banani   55
Photograph 7.   Participants from the Korail focus group   57
Photograph 8.   The completion of the Mirpur group seasonal chart   62
Photograph 9.   Waste pickers in the Korail *bustee*   69
Photograph 10.   Jussna and friend, pickers at the Matuail landfill site 73

Tables

Table 1.	SLA core concepts	7
Table 2.	Summary of wet season effects	14
Table 3.	Ranking exercise results	42
Table 4.	Research areas for individual participants	54
Table 5.	Details of individual participants	54
Table 6.	Focus group areas	57

Glossary

Bustee	Slum
Bangla	The national language of Bangladesh and mother tongue of all research participants.
Dealer	In the context of this report, a dealer is an individual to whom waste pickers sell their valuable waste after collection.
Eid	Islamic festival falling twice a year.
Livelihood	A livelihood comprises the means, activities, entitlements and assets by which people make a living. (See also below.)
Taka (Tk)	The currency in Bangladesh. At time of writing there were approximately Tk50 to US$1.00, Tk80 to UK £1.00.
Tokai	Bangla word for waste picker
Waste picker	An individual who collects and sells valuable waste as a livelihood.

Sustainable Livelihood

The following is a definition of sustainable *rural* livelihoods as defined by DFID. This is valuable (albeit in need of some adaptation) in understanding the nature of a sustainable urban livelihood.

> 'A livelihood comprises the capabilities, assets (including both material and social resources) and activities required for a means of living. A livelihood is sustainable when it can cope with and recover from stresses and shocks and maintain or enhance its capabilities and assets both now and in the future, while not undermining the natural resource base.' (Carney, 1998: 4)

Background

The UK Department for International Development (DFID) Sustainable Livelihoods Approach (SLA) was originally developed as a means by which to study rural people's livelihoods. The objective of this research was to evaluate the SLA as a practical framework for understanding the livelihoods of, and ultimately helping, waste pickers in the *urban* setting of Dhaka.

The research was based entirely on practical field work and participatory research with waste pickers. There were three outputs from the research, as follows:

■ An understanding of how the SLA performed in this urban situation;

■ A set of detailed livelihood profiles of a sample of waste pickers in Dhaka, and an increased general understanding of their work and lives; and

■ A number of lessons learned about the practical approach to livelihood research.

These are described in the course of this booklet using examples and case studies drawn from the work in Dhaka.

How this booklet is organised

This booklet is divided into two parts. Part I: Key Findings presents the livelihood-related findings for waste pickers and draws a number of conclusions about the nature, vulnerability and sustainability of their livelihoods. The performance of the SLA as a research tool in the urban setting is also discussed in this section.

Part II: Field Notes describes the fieldwork methodology and highlights some of the lessons learned and pitfalls encountered during research. This section describes a number of the participatory techniques employed, and raises general issues about research with illiterate, underprivileged children.

More detailed outlines can be found at the beginning of Parts I and II.

Part I: Key findings

Outline

This part of the booklet is a presentation of the key findings from the livelihoods research with waste pickers in Dhaka.

The first section provides background information to the research and describes waste pickers and the SLA in more detail. The following six sections are structured around the framework of the sustainable livelihood approach itself. The sections cover vulnerability contexts, asset profiles, transforming structures and processes and livelihood strategies and outcomes. Section 8 summarises and discusses the findings, and Section 9 proposes scope for future livelihood research with waste pickers.

1.
Introduction

1.1 Why research waste pickers in Dhaka?

Bangladesh is a poor country and Dhaka represents a typical urban centre. Pickers are invariably slum-dwellers or are homeless on the streets. They enjoy little (if any) access to health services, education or legal aid of any form. In addition, they are perceived as having very low status in society and are strongly associated with criminals. They are considered and treated as public nuisances. As such, this was a study of some of the most underprivileged and marginalized inhabitants of Dhaka.

Many waste pickers originate from rural areas. This makes them of particular interest because they may have experience of seeking livelihoods in both urban and rural areas. Their experience can aid the understanding of the relevance of rural livelihood research techniques in the urban context as well as the differences between the nature of such livelihoods themselves.

Very little has been written about the livelihoods of waste pickers in Dhaka, particularly from a 'sustainable livelihoods' viewpoint. This research sought to respond to the need for understanding pickers' livelihoods and the problems they face. A detailed level of under-standing is vital for effective integration of the agenda of the poor into existing sector-based approaches to development. In addition, there is a shortage of written material relating to practical sustainable livelihoods research in the urban setting. It is hoped that this booklet will help bridge the gap between academic research and practical experience in the field.

Although this research enjoyed full co-operation from local collaborators and waste pickers, the extent to which there existed a local demand for research on poverty and livelihood related issues was not clear. Most NGO work in Dhaka is still sector-based, and poverty alleviation has not been mainstreamed. Because of the poverty-focus of this research, it could be argued that its greatest supporters would be its primary stakeholders, the poor themselves.

1.2 Who are waste pickers?

Dhaka is a city with a population of around seven million and a grave solid waste problem. Dhaka City Corporation, responsible for solid waste management, has limited resources, which means it is unable to remove all waste generated daily (Kazi 1999). As a result, in most areas the streets are strewn with waste, skips for transporting waste to landfill sites are overflowing and drains (sewers) are blocked by discarded plastic. While many people in Dhaka find this a disgusting inconvenience and health risk there is a group of people who, while they may share these views, seek and find a livelihood in this ubiquitous resource.

Photograph 1. Pickers carrying waste at Matuail landfill

Waste pickers in Dhaka operate throughout the city picking valuable waste from the streets, from communal street dumps and from municipal authority's skips and landfill sites. They collect paper, plastics, glass, bones and metals. Some collect fuel for cooking, and some even collect food for themselves. Pickers sell their valuable waste to 'dealers' situated in the bazaars or in their *bustees* (slums). Most work early in the morning and some continue throughout the day.

While it is possible to find male and female pickers of all ages in Dhaka, the majority are young boys between the ages of around seven and fourteen years. The work is unpleasant, and frequently the areas in which waste is found are used as public latrines. The health and safety problems associated with the work are numerous and many are obvious.

Waste pickers are frequently referred to as 'pickers' in this report. On occasion, they are also generalised as male. This is mostly for linguistic simplicity and because the majority of pickers in Dhaka are boys.

1.3 The sustainable livelihoods approach

1.3.1 SLA in brief

The DFID SLA Guidance Sheets (1999) describe a sustainable livelihood as follows;

> *'A livelihood comprises the capabilities, assets (including both material and social resources) and activities required for a means of living. A livelihood is sustainable when it can cope with and recover from stresses and shocks and maintain or enhance its capabilities and assets both now and into the future, while not undermining its resource base.' (DFID 1999: 1.1)*

In addition to availability of and access to waste, a picker's livelihood may be said to comprise good health, ability to work and supportive social environment and infrastructure.

> *'The sustainable livelihoods approach ... has been developed to help understand and analyse the livelihoods of the poor. [The framework] endeavours to provide a way of thinking about the livelihoods of poor people that will stimulate debate and reflection, thereby improving performance of poverty reduction.' (DFID 1999: 1.1)*

The SLA was originally developed as a means by which to study rural people's livelihoods. The model has been adapted by various organisations, and the SLA model used for this research was that developed and defined by the UK Department for International Development (DFID). The DFID SLA takes an holistic view of the factors that cause poverty. These include vulnerabilities, lack of assets, institutional inadequacies and lack of access to services. The approach is intended to deepen understanding of livelihoods and expose those aspects that are unsustainable or vulnerable. This in turn is intended to enable the formulation of more incisive, better-informed practical responses, to make livelihoods more sustainable and resilient. The approach itself is not described in detail in this report. Some level of pre-existing knowledge will aid the reader in understanding certain issues but is not necessary.

1.3.2 Core concepts

The SLA examines the livelihood in four broad, and occasionally overlapping, sections. These are intended to cover all aspects of, and forces on, a livelihood. Table 1 is compiled from information in the DFID livelihoods guidance sheets (DFID 1999) and provides a brief explanation of the core concepts of the SLA.

Table 1. SLA core concepts	
Concept	*Outline*
Vulnerability context	This 'frames the external environment in which people exist. People's livelihoods and the wider availability of assets are fundamentally affected by critical **trends** as well as by **shocks** and **seasonality** – over which they have limited or no control.'
Livelihood assets	The study of livelihood assets 'seeks to gain an accurate and realistic understanding of people's strengths (assets or capital endowments) and how they endeavour to convert these into positive livelihood outcomes. The approach is founded on a belief that people require a range of assets to achieve positive livelihood outcomes; no single category of assets on its own is sufficient to yield all the many and varied livelihood outcomes that people seek.' The study of assets is broken down into categories of human, social, natural, physical and financial capitals.
Transforming structures and processes	'Transforming structures and processes within the livelihoods framework are the institutions, organisations, policies and legislation that shape livelihoods.' The SLA examines them in terms of the effect they have on livelihood assets and the degree to which they include or exclude a group of people and provide them with a sense of well-being.
Livelihood strategies and outcomes	*Strategies* is 'the overarching term used to denote the range and combination of activities and choices that people make/undertake in order to achieve their livelihood goals.' The SLA seeks to promote choice, opportunity and diversity. *Outcomes* are 'the achievements or outputs of *Livelihood Strategies.*' It must be recognised that the outcomes that people pursue may be very different from those of the researcher.

1.3.3 SLA performance criteria

Using the SLA as a basis for fieldwork and research will always raise certain issues relating to the effectiveness, appropriateness and relevance of the approach. However, use of the SLA in an urban context is likely to raise specific issues resulting from the fact that the SLA was originally developed as a rural tool. This was very much in mind in the course of this research, and this booklet describes some of the problems encountered in the rural-urban translation of the framework.

The SLA is assessed for its suitability for this research in the light of the following four criteria:

1.   How incisive?
2.   How relevant?
3.   How appropriate? and
4.   How comprehensive?

These are touched on throughout the booklet and discussed in detail in Section 7.

2.
Vulnerability context

2.1 Shocks

'Shocks can destroy assets directly ... or force people to abandon their home areas and dispose of assets. Recent events have highlighted the impact that international economic shocks, including rapid changes in exchange rates or terms of trade, can have on the very poor.' (DFID 1999. 2.2)

The nature of shocks to which pickers are vulnerable are quite different from those of a rural farmer. The most marked difference relates to the resources required for their respective livelihoods. Farmers may face problems with crop damage or theft, sudden drops in market prices or decreases in availability or access to certain resources such as water. By contrast, pickers' one tangible resource (i.e. waste) is not liable to damage, theft, supply problems or, according to this research, unexpected changes in market value. The nature of the livelihoods themselves also affects the shock vulnerability. For example, waste pickers primarily work alone, and are solely responsible for the success of their work and each day is critical. Agricultural work however is undertaken by teams, and working at specific times may not be so critical. For example, if a picker is ill for a day his income suffers, while if a farmer is ill for a few days (particularly at certain times in the year) this may have no impact on his income or security.

Pickers are vulnerable to certain shocks, some of which are discussed below.

2.1.1 Health shocks

The research found that most shocks to pickers were associated with the health of individuals and their families. Illness may result in a picker being unable to work for a period, which results in a loss of earnings. In addition, ill health can necessitate expenditure on medical treatment which, set against a pickers' income, is high. The participant Muman reported paying Tk100 (US$2) for medicine to treat a fever that had prevented him for working for three days. His daily income was Tk50. A family member suffering ill-health can necessitate an expensive trip to a home village or the reduction in livelihood activities to allow more time for care.

Few pickers considered their work dangerous and, in contrast to the widely held opinion that they frequently hurt themselves whilst picking through waste, few mentioned any work-related accidents. Some said they had sustained injuries, and these were mostly cuts which they did not consider to be serious. This may be an issue of perspective and knowledge on hygiene and health issues, which is likely to be limited. Perhaps the same cut from glass covered in organic waste, or rusted metal would cause alarm in others better informed.

One region in which picking activity is undoubtedly more dangerous than others is the Matuail landfill site. Here the pickers not only have dangers from treading on and sorting through the waste (often with no shoes, and never gloves), but also from the mechanical diggers amongst which they move. Jussna's Mother was killed in an accident with one of the diggers. Despite this, she said she did not consider the work particularly dangerous. Photograph 2 shows pickers sorting waste as it is being shifted and exposed by a mechanical digger at the Matuail landfill site in Dhaka.

Photograph 2. Pickers around the diggers at Matuail landfill

2.1.2 Other shocks

Shocks to homes

Other shocks that pickers face involve their homes. The Korail *bustee* is typical of slums in which pickers live in Dhaka. It is situated on land owned by the government, and like many slums before it, is liable to be destroyed at any time to make way for building development. Some pickers spoke of this uncertainty. There are frequent reports of 'illegal' slums being demolished by government bulldozers, the inhabitants having been given no warning for fear of instigating riots.

Fire also poses a threat to bustees. Since the research took place, a newspaper reported that a fire spread through the Begum Bari area where Jushim and Raju lived, razing some 10,000 slum dwellings to the ground, leaving perhaps 40,000 homeless. Most inhabitants reported losing everything to the fire or the subsequent looting.[1] It is not known what action was taken to assist these people, if any.

Families in slums are among the worst hit during storms because the buildings are so insubstantial. *Bustees* are also often situated on low land making them more susceptible to flooding.

Marriages and funerals
The funeral of a family member or the marriage of a son or daughter could also be considered a shock, and incur significant expense to families. Most of the participants in this research are either too young or independent from families for this to be an issue. However, the one older female participant, Maleka (age 35) reported that she had had to borrow large sums of money for the marriage of her two daughters.

Personal safety
Some of the dangers that could be considered shocks to pickers include kidnap and beatings. Saddam said he feared kidnap and being sold as a slave, and Shafi reported beatings by guards due to his being considered a thief by virtue of being a picker. Others, such as Muman, fear being falsely accused of a crime and arrested by the police.

2.1.3 Coping mechanisms
If a picker does not have sufficient money at hand to pay for medicine or travel etc. he or she needs to either use savings or borrow the money. Three of the pickers interviewed did save money, and Muman used savings he kept with a bazaar stall-holder to pay for his medicine. Those who have no savings would be most likely to turn to family for help, or borrow money from friends or the dealers to whom they sell their waste. Dealers may also lend money for weddings, funerals, trips to villages and even investments in small businesses. It is an important contingency for pickers in times of unexpected need.

Pickers appear to have little (if any) recourse to the law, ranging from the police service to the judicial system or legal aid. The officials at the Farm Gate Aparajeyo hostel for street children said that generally homeless children avoid moving or sleeping in certain areas which they know are liable to kidnappings or police raids.

A number of these issues are revisited later in this booklet. Section 3.5 describes some of the financial contingencies of pickers, and Section 3.2.2 describes the relationship between pickers and their dealers in more detail. Issues relating to the police service and their dealings with pickers are discussed in Section 4.1.

Clearly, the shocks to which urban pickers are susceptible are more based on human than natural assets. The health, safety and homes of pickers appear to be the more vulnerable aspects of their livelihoods. Understanding existing coping mechanisms for dealing with these shocks is likely to be a good starting point from which to devise ways of helping pickers increase their resilience. This is an important area to further examine in the livelihoods of pickers and exposes some important vulnerabilities.

2.2 Trends

'Trends may (or may not) be more benign [than shocks], though they are more predictable. They have a particularly important influence on rates of return (economic or otherwise) to chosen livelihood strategies.' (DFID 1999, 2.2)

Only two pickers mentioned trends in any aspect of their picking activities and both were associated with industrial waste in the Begum Bari area. Jushim said he used to be able to pick more biscuit wrappers from the factory, but now more of them are sold on direct to dealers. The second trend was described by Raju. Like most pickers interviewed, he reported no change in the number of pickers in the local area but a general increase in the amount of waste, in part due to the increased activities of industry.

There are a number of possible reasons why so little data on trends was gathered. There is, of course, the possibility that no trends exist, or that the participants do not wish (for whatever reasons) to speak about them. There is also the aspect of age. Many of the participants were young and have had limited experience of past years and are therefore unable to comment. It is interesting that the only boy who mentioned a longer-term trend (over one year) was one of the older participants (Raju who, at the age of fourteen, has been picking for seven years). While the lack of trends and the reticence and age of participants are likely to account for some of the shortage of trend data, it is possible there is another more subtle reason. This involves trends combining in such a way that their effects are negated. This makes them 'invisible' to the picker and researcher alike. 'Invisible trends' are explored further in the 'Field Notes' booklet.

2.3 Seasonality

'Seasonal shifts in prices, employment opportunities and food availability are one of the greatest and most enduring sources of hardship for poor people in developing countries.' (DFID 1999, 2.2)

The study of seasonal trends in waste pickers' lives and livelihoods led to some of the most important findings in the research.

Seasons were discussed with each individual participant, and constituted a major part of the *focus group* work. The research showed that waste pickers are affected by seasons, that in general their lives are easier during the dryer and cooler periods of the year, and that a 'lean period' exists for many during the wet season. The results of discussion with individuals were qualitative while the findings of the two group sessions were more quantitative. Contradictions existed both within and between each set of findings. They are discussed individually in the following sections.

2.3.1 Individual participant findings

Compared to the findings from the two *focus group* sessions, discussions with individual pickers revealed relatively sparse seasonal information. In individual interviews, pickers said most about the wet months (described below) and relatively little about the other seasons. Only Nasir pointed out that he found work tiring in the hot dry season but said he became accustomed to it, and a few boys mentioned that in the hotter seasons they were able to find more plastic mineral water bottles. Raju and his dealer Abdul Jumna said that house repair causes an increase in amount of waste available, which they said occurred in the hot season. No reference was made to the cold season in any of the individual interviews.

Other 'seasonal' factors that affect waste are religious occasions. Eid was mentioned as a time when generally more valuable waste (particularly bones) was available. This was found to be particularly marked at the Matuail dump.

The wet season

The wet season in Bangladesh lasts from May to August and is characterised by extensive flooding and high humidity and temperatures. Table 2 below summarises some of the information gathered from the nine individually interviewed participants. Not all pickers commented on every aspect.

Nearly all individual participants commented that picking was more unpleasant a task during the wet season than at dry times due to the rain. Rain soils the waste with a sludge of vegetation and makes the pickers themselves feel cold – despite the heat. In addition, the rain spoils the paper, which makes it difficult to collect and lowers its value.

There was little agreement regarding the effect of the rains on incomes and amount of waste available. These discrepancies and contradictions could be accounted for by the small sample interviewed, by incorrect information being provided in interviews, or by actual differences in the way different pickers are affected by the rain.[2] This introduces the danger of considering pickers as one consistent group, as well as the possibility that the nature of waste, waste pickers and seasonal trends vary regionally. Regional variation in waste is discussed shortly.

Table 2. Summary of wet season effect		
Aspect	**Effect**	**No. of responses**
Quantity of waste	Up	3
	Down	1
	No different	1
Cannot pick paper	-	3
Income	Up	4
	Down	2
Work more unpleasant	-	6

2.3.2 Focus group seasonality charts

Seasonality research was also undertaken with the two focus groups in Dhaka, in Mirpur and the Korail *bustee*. Details of the exercises carried out are described in Part II, Section 3.2 Articulation and group work. One exercise was the completion of a seasonal chart using picture cards and seeds to indicate changes in a number of factors in the course of a year. Photograph 3 shows the seasonal chart as completed by a group of pickers in the Mirpur hostel.

Figures 1 and 2 are graphical representations of the seasonal trends indicated on the charts by the Mirpur and Korail focus groups respectively. Darker shading indicates more seeds, white indicates no seeds. In the health row;

- ☺ indicates good health;
- ☻ indicates average health; and,
- ☹ indicates poor health.

In the Food row, a fat man indicates plenty of food, and a thin man indicates a shortage of food. Areas left blank indicate a 'normal' food situation.

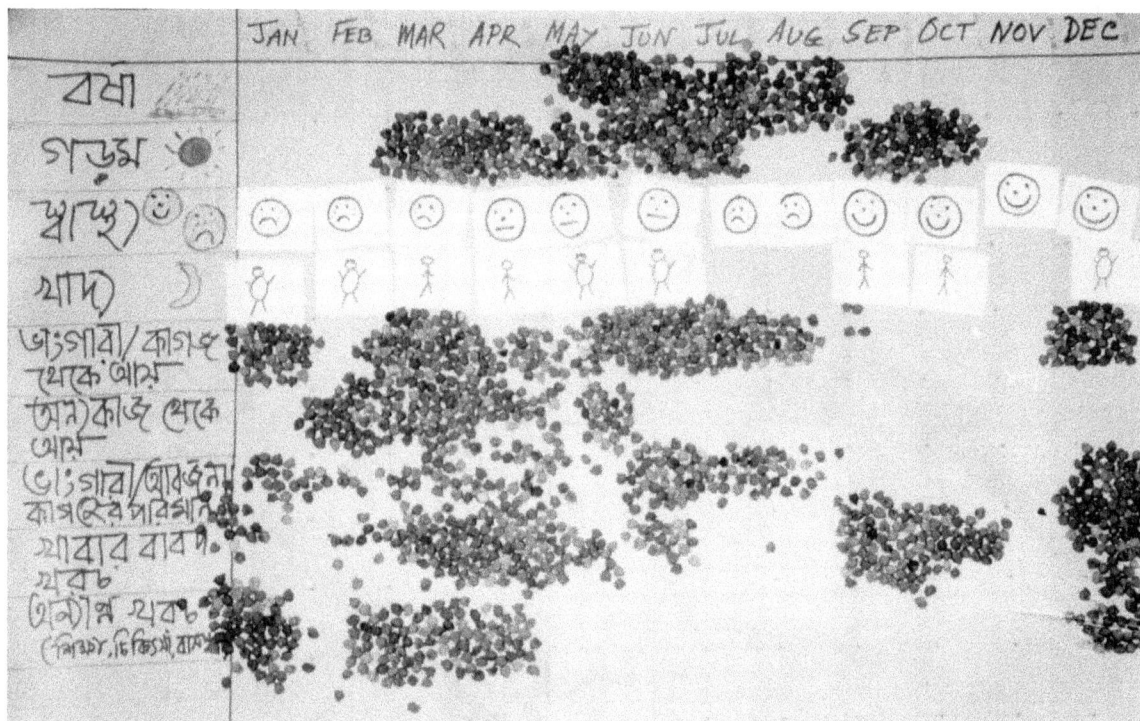

Photograph 3. Mirpur Group Seasonal Chart

The seasonal chart for the Korail *bustee* group was simplified by virtue of the lower level of education and literacy of participants, and in response to lessons learned from the first focus group in Mirpur.

During the completion of the charts by the pickers, they were asked to qualify some of the trends they had indicated. However, because the purpose of this exercise was for them to be left-alone to complete the charts with as little help or guidance from facilitators as possible, these discussions were kept to a minimum. Sometimes the questions appeared to help them think issues through while at other times the questions were distracting. The following summarises their responses.

The Mirpur group introduced the effects of the rice harvests on their seasonal charts. In April and October they considered themselves to be least well off with food because they are immediately before the rice harvests (it is assumed that there is a shortage of rice at these times which may result in higher prices). They also attributed high expenditure in February to the high prices of the first harvest of the year's vegetables. Trends in waste were attributed to a number of detailed factors. The two Muslim Eid festivals fell in January and March in 2000, and these resulted in an increase in quantity and value of waste, and hence picking income. In addition, in March they could find many more drinks cans which have a high market value.

Figure 1. Mirpur hostel seasonal chart

	Jan	Feb	Mar	Apr	May	Jun	Jul	Aug	Sep	Oct	Nov	Dec
Heat												
Rain												
Health	☹	☹	☹	🙂	🙂	🙂	☹	☹	🙂	🙂	🙂	🙂
Food & nutrition												
Picking Incomes												
Other Incomes												
Waste trends												
Food Expenditure												
Other Expenditure												

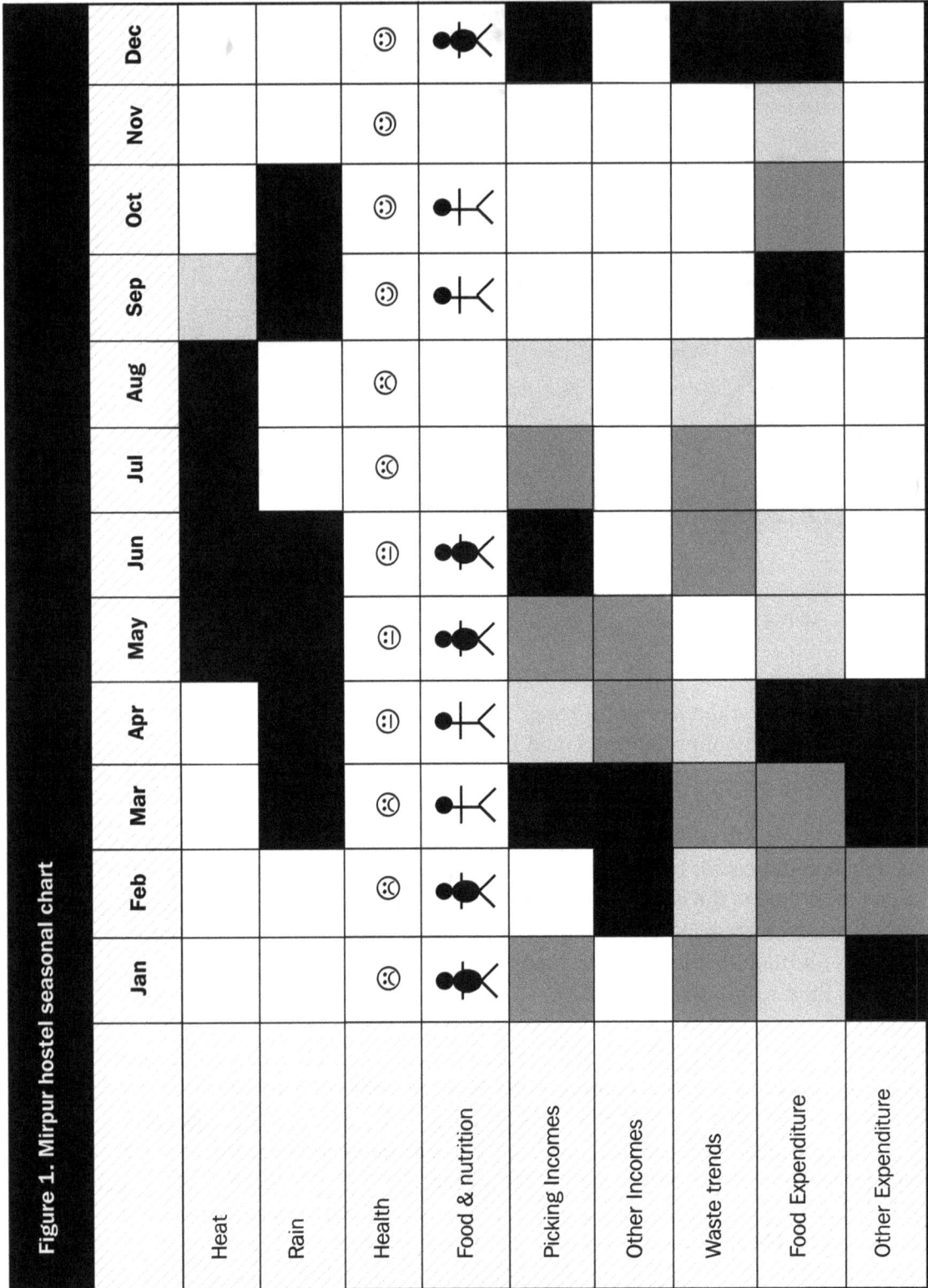

Key: Dark shading indicates more seeds, lighter shading indicates fewer seeds, blank squares contained no seeds.

Figure 2. Korail *bustee* seasonal chart			
	Hot and dry	*Hot and rainy*	*Cold and dry*
Health	☹	☺	☺
Food and Nutrition		🧍	🧍
Amount of waste			
Income from waste			
Other income			
General expenditure			
Helping parents			

NB. All seasons and rows were represented by pictures. See Figure 4 for examples.

'Other incomes' applied to three boys only and were derived from ice cream selling during the hotter months of the year.

The Korail *bustee* shows a number of interesting trends which were qualified by discussions with the participants. Their health was generally considered to be poorer during the hot season because they suffered from diarrhoea, lack of sleep, dehydration, scabies and jaundice. Food in the hot season was described as acceptable (though one participant did comment on the speed at which it went off), but the best season for food was when it was coldest. The rains were said to badly affect their diets. They said it is difficult to travel to buy food because of flooding, and wood for cooking becomes difficult to find and heavier to carry. Expenditure was average in the dry season and high in the wet season due to higher food prices (due to scarcity) and because they spend money repairing their houses. They also spend more time helping their parents during the rains (particularly helping to repair houses), as well as during the hot dry season.

Comparison of the charts

It is clear that while there are many similarities between the charts, certain quite fundamental differences exist between data, such as an inversion of opinions about when there is more or less waste. Some of the similarities and differences between the charts can be accounted for (correctly or otherwise) on account of the circumstances of the pickers in the respective groups. Health and availability of food affected both groups similarly; both ate and felt best during the cool dry season, and suffered most illness during the hot dry season. However, the higher prices of food during the wet season (mentioned by both groups) had a more marked effect on the poorer Korail group who did not have a hostel to provide food and relied on their families. The Korail *bustee* group went without food during this period, and paid higher prices for that which they did buy (expenditure was highest during the wet season for Korail *bustee* group). The Mirpur boys pay a daily fee to the hostel for their keep, and so are unaffected by seasonal price changes. Their expenditure trends revolved around religious periods such as Eid.

Focus group summary

Further trends, similarities and differences could be highlighted from these findings but in order to do so meaningfully, data from many more similar groups would need to be examined.

The trends highlighted demonstrate that seasonal charting can be an effective tool for clarifying the activities of, and effect of seasons on, different groups of pickers. The results of the focus group also demonstrate the ability of young children to distil and articulate their ideas when given the correct facilities and environment to do so. The abilities of the (often uneducated) young participants in this research must not be underestimated or undervalued.

2.3.3 Regional variation of seasonality

The findings show clear discrepancies in how the amount of waste available for picking varies during the year. If it is assumed that pickers are, to the best of their knowledge, providing accurate information, the amount of waste itself may be varying with the seasons in different ways, *in different locations*.

Raju in Begum Bari stated that during the wet season waste is reportedly liberated from ponds (areas of water about ¼ acre in size) by rain thus increasing the amount of waste available. It is not clear exactly how this process occurs, but a participant in the Korail *bustee* Focus Group also drew a distinction between areas with ponds and areas where there are no ponds. He said there is less waste available in the latter during the rains. This is one example of spatial variation in seasonal effects on waste quantities.

A second example also exists in Begum Bari, the area of Dhaka chosen because of the presence of industry. In contrast to other areas in Dhaka, Raju and Jushim described the access they had to certain sources of valuable waste from the local industries. The valuable waste included iron (usually in powdered form) from a smelting plant, rags and clothes from garment factories, plastic from bangle manufacturers and wrappers from a biscuit factory.

While these comprised an estimated 30% of Raju's income, no such waste was reportedly found in any of the residential areas.

The existence of spatial variation in nature and quantities of waste introduces the need to move away from conceptualising pickers as a single consistent group. In order to be certain of what accounts for apparent regional variation, cross-checking is a useful and important tool. This is described in Part II Section 4.5.

2.3.4 Reliance on picking activities

The incomes that pickers derive from waste during the wet season appears to be in part dependent upon the extent to which they *rely* on picking for their own survival. For example, Shafi and Shahib Ali rely entirely on waste picking for their survival, and they both said that they had no option but to continue picking during the wet season in order to pay hostel fees and survive. Most other pickers had families who could help support them, and chose not to work during the rains when they found picking more unpleasant. All the pickers in the Korail *bustee* had families.

This difference amongst waste pickers serves to reinforce the need to recognise different groups, in different areas, amongst pickers.

2.4 Vulnerability summary

This section has discussed pickers' vulnerability to shocks, trends and seasonality. The nature of health, safety, housing and financial shocks have been outlined as well as some of the mechanisms employed to cope with them. The lack of trend information (and possible reasons for this) has been discussed, and the few trends that pickers mentioned have been outlined. Results of enquiries relating to seasonality have been presented, from individuals, groups and waste dealers in turn. These led to two tentative conclusions being drawn about pickers and waste: the spatial variability of seasonal effects, and the fact that different pickers' personal circumstances affect the way in which they respond to climatic changes.

The study of vulnerabilities has also highlighted a number of points worthy of consideration in further research and involvement with waste pickers in Dhaka and elsewhere. These are summarised below.

- It is not possible to treat all waste pickers as a single consistent group.
- Meticulous methodology and cross-checking is vital for gathering and checking accurate findings.
- A large sample is required for building an accurate and meaningful picture of livelihoods of waste pickers.
- Group work is a tool that can be used to good effect with young participants and is likely to be key in obtaining accurate findings.

The SLA has provided a useful and thorough basis for investigating the vulnerabilities and coping methods of waste pickers. It is clear that a close examination of this aspect of livelihoods can shed light on issues vital in appreciating the lives, livelihood processes and general wellbeing of individuals throughout the annual cycle.

3.
Asset profiles

The SLA seeks to empower people to help themselves through building on what they already have. In order to achieve this, a detailed understanding of people's existing assets must be developed. The SLA systematically tackles each of five types of assets; Human, Social, Natural, Physical and Financial. These are discussed in the light of research findings and observations in the following five sub-sections.

3.1 Human capital
DFID objective:
> *'Improved access to high-quality education, information, technologies and training and better nutrition and health'. (DFID 1999)*

3.1.1 General findings
Human capital is not the greatest asset for waste pickers. In terms of pursuing their present livelihoods, pickers are sufficiently endowed with 'human capital', but in terms of being able to *improve* or change their livelihoods, they are lacking.

Most pickers interviewed considered themselves adequately endowed with the skills necessary for carrying out their job. Indeed, most considered that little or no skill was required. This is clearly not the case, and may be indicative of a low opinion they hold of themselves and their livelihoods. Pickers know the value of different types of waste, where to find it, where to sell it and who to sell it to. They know to sell in bulk rather than daily in order to get higher prices. Pickers also understand the opportunity cost of their time and effort in terms of what waste to pick; metals may be harder to find but more valuable, while discarded paper is ubiquitous and easy to find but sells for much less.

3.1.2 Education
Many pickers interviewed said that they could not afford to attend school. However, in Bangladesh, primary education is officially freely available to all.[3] It seems the prohibitive cost of schooling is not high fees but lost earning opportunities. These lost earnings can be

referred to as the opportunity cost. Many of the pickers live 'hand to mouth', have no savings and cannot withstand a drop in income.

There are some other possible reasons for the low school attendance. Reasons of opportunity cost may be seen as inconsistent with the fact that most pickers do not pick all day every day, just in the mornings. It could therefore be argued that pickers could attend afternoon sessions without impacting their work. However, accessible schools may not have afternoon sessions, and picking waste is most rewarding early in the morning. Other reasons may include a lack of schooling facilities in *bustee* areas, issues relating to their status or just an inability to buy school provisions. Whatever the reasons, pickers' lack of access to the education system means that their prospects for getting better paid jobs are limited. Further research is required to be certain of the reasons.

3.1.3 Training opportunities

In the same way as education, opportunities for training for semi-skilled jobs do exist, but pickers are held back by the opportunity cost of the time they would take. The following two examples from Dhaka illustrate this.

Box 1. Training opportunities

Sari looms in Mirpur area. In walking around Mirpur it is clear that there are many hundreds of buildings full of sari weaving looms operated by children. The conditions of work do not look too bad, and in comparison to picking work, at the very least cleaner. At the end of the Focus Group in Mirpur, the boys were asked why they continued waste picking when they could work in the looms. They explained that this was not an option for them, as extensive training would be required, and they could not afford to give the time because of their schooling.

The garments industry in Begum Bari area. Raju, a picker in Begum Bari, said that he would like to stop picking and start work in the clothes-making industry, a ubiquitous and large employer in the area. However, because of initial training needs he would suffer a drop in income until he had learned the necessary skills. At present, he said his family were facing financial difficulties and that, although the salary would soon exceed what he was earning through picking, they could not withstand this temporary drop.[5]

It seems that many pickers would be able to take up training opportunities if they could spare the time (in Mirpur it is being 'invested' in education) and were able to withstand the shock of a temporary drop in income (which many cannot). In addition, by virtue of undertaking the training, pickers would be expecting to change their occupation and stop picking activities, so they may no longer be able to borrow money from their dealers (see Section 3.2.2 for more details on this relationship). According to dealers and pickers, few alternative credit sources exist, so this constitutes a further disincentive to undertake training. This is an example of how different parts of livelihoods overlap. The way in which parts of the livelihoods approach overlap is one of its strengths, and part of how it achieves its holistic approach.

3.1.4 Reducing opportunity cost

The issues raised above highlight the prohibitively high opportunity cost of time spent increasing stock of 'human capital', which can facilitate an improvement in occupation as well as an increase in salary. The opportunity cost could be reduced by providing ways to enable pickers to continue to support themselves and their families through periods of reduced or zero salary. This could be achieved by providing loans or grants, or education and training opportunities that can be pursued alongside their picking activities.

Many jobs are better paid than picking, and most enjoy a higher associated status. Giving pickers the freedom and opportunity to choose other jobs, including those requiring training, directly fulfils the DFID objective for livelihood strategies.

3.1.5 Technology and tools

The only two tools that waste pickers use are a metal spike for turning waste over in dumps, and a plastic sack. While technology could not offer much to help them in their present occupations, availability of affordable technology could enable them to change or modify their livelihoods. One such example is a 'tricycle-van'; a cycle rickshaw with a container instead of a seat on the back, such that are used by 'door-to-door collectors'. The merits of this livelihood alternative are described in Section 3.3.4. In terms of improving or changing livelihoods, pickers appear to have a need for, but little access to, technology, and this is in part due again to prohibitive cost. Ways in which pickers are able to meet the costs of everyday living, and improve their livelihoods through investment are explored in the following section.

3.1.6 Health care

Information on the health care available to pickers is scant, and more work would be required to build a detailed understanding of the nature of and access to the health care they enjoy.

Reports on the extent to which free (government) health services are available to pickers vary. Muman and Shahib Ali reported having to pay substantial amounts for medical treatment (to treat fever and mental illness respectively). Other pickers said that they could receive certain treatment for free. Raju, for example, cut himself and was able to get the wound stitched freely. He said the only charges for medical treatment were for drugs. In terms of health care the Mirpur boys are exceptional in that they enjoy access to health care from the hostel.

Illness can not only cost earnings, but it can cause individuals and families to have to choose between heavy debt and life.

3.1.7 Summary

Pickers generally have few transferable, marketable skills, and the 'opportunity cost' of time spent training may be prohibitively high. Many pickers are trapped in their occupations, and this is exacerbated by the 'poverty ratchet' effect whereby the more needy are those least able to help themselves.

The DFID objective of improved access to high-quality education, information, technologies, training and better nutrition and health is far from being realised for waste pickers. This section has highlighted something of the extent to which waste pickers are marginalised, a theme revisited later in this booklet. The key to empowering them to improve or change their livelihoods lies in understanding their lack of, and helping them to improve, their stocks of human capital. Assistance could be offered by working towards more inclusive high level policy as well as by helping to make the opportunity cost of training or education more affordable.

3.2 Social capital

DFID objective:
> *Development of 'a more supportive and cohesive social environment'. (DFID 1999:2.3.2)*

3.2.1 General findings

The study of social capital is vital for understanding the ways in which waste pickers use friends and family in their livelihoods and cope with shocks. Pickers in Dhaka lack access to the formal infrastructure and services of the country, so their social networks constitute their 'safety nets'. In times of need pickers first turn either to their families, friends or wider communities for practical and financial help. Similarly, because pickers do not feel they could ever turn to the police, in situations where safety or personal property is threatened (or perhaps justice required) social networks are again the main recourse.[6]

In addition to constituting safety nets, social relationships also impact livelihoods. Many pickers work in pairs for social reasons and because they say they feel safer. Shafi said that he found his dealer through a friend's recommendation, and other boys, such as Muman, learnt about picking from older brothers or friends.

Pickers usually live in specific areas, either on the streets or in *bustees*. Detailed studies of the communities in which pickers live have not been undertaken in this research. However, within these areas three main sets of relations are known to exist which are relevant to waste pickers. The first such is the family who, according to many pickers, are called upon before any others in times of difficulty. The second set of relationships is friends. The third is those existing between pickers and their dealers.

In the absence of family, Muman who lives alone on the streets in Dhaka says that if he was in any difficulty he would turn to his friends. They would offer him what help they could, including money. Most of the other pickers also confirmed this in what they said.

3.2.2 Relationship with dealers

The relationship between dealers became known in this research primarily as a result of discussions about money. When asked to whom they would turn for money if in crisis, many pickers said that they would consider turning to the dealer to whom they sold their waste. Dealers were also consulted about this and they confirmed that they regularly provide credit to pickers. The system is regulated by a symbiotic relationship of trust, and 'interest' is paid not in money, but by loyalty.

Dealers reported that they would lend money to pickers for various reasons including travel back to a home village, medicines and religious festivals. Repayments could be made either in cash, or, more likely in valuable waste. When asked about interest, Tahajudin echoed the answers of all dealers in his response; 'Loyalty is my interest'. In return for offering loans, dealers expect to be brought all the waste picked by borrowers. Both parties have benefited. The dealer has secured a monopoly on a particular picker, and the picker has been able to deal with a crisis without sinking deep into debt with a money lender, or going without.

Much of this relationship relies on trust. When Jakeel Hussein, a dealer in the Korail *bustee*, was asked what he would do if a picker failed to repay his loans, he said; 'We are all poor here. Sometimes people cannot pay, and that is that. There is nothing we can do.' Riyadge, a dealer at Matuail stated that this was his philosophy too. It is important to note that this relationship does not appear to be exploitative. Some data regarding buying and selling prices of waste was collected from pickers and their respective dealers. Assuming pickers and (particularly) dealers were providing correct information, this data also indicated that dealers were not exploiting the pickers and were usually quite poor themselves.

3.3 Natural capital

DFID objective:
> *'More secure access to, and better management of, natural resources'. (DFID 1999:2.3.3)*

Natural capital is the asset that translates least readily from the rural to urban context. It is also the asset for which the Sustainable Livelihoods Approach requires most modification to become relevant for waste pickers.

3.3.1 DFID natural capital livelihoods objectives

In addition to stating the natural capital livelihoods objectives, the DFID sustainable livelihoods guidance sheets also provide examples of ways in which this can be achieved. These examples refer to *rural* livelihood interventions and relate to *rural* forms of natural capital.

Specific references to rural activities (e.g. farming and biodiversity) will not be relevant to pickers, but there are certain *concepts* which are also not relevant. The following bullet points outline the intervention possibilities DFID cites. Each possibility is then discussed in the light of pickers' livelihood activities and their natural capital, which is assumed to be waste. References to farming activities in the DFID text have been replaced by 'waste picking'.

- ***DFID suggested intervention: Direct support to asset accumulation,*** *through conservation of resources and provision of services / inputs for [waste picking].*

  Assuming waste is a picker's natural capital, natural asset accumulation is a concept that is not relevant, except perhaps in terms of storing waste to sell in bulk. In terms of specific services / inputs described in the guidance sheets it is possible that certain services could be useful to pickers, but services and inputs which increased the amount of accessible waste may not be universally popular.

- ***DFID suggested intervention: Indirect support (through Transforming Structures and Processes)*** *through changes in organisations and institutions concerned with waste management and access control, environmental legislation and support to market development.*

  It is clear that all but one of these would negatively impact the livelihood of a waste picker. 'Changes in institutions that manage, and govern access to, natural resources' could only logically mean 'improvements' in waste management, and 'Environmental legislation and enforcement mechanisms' would most likely lead to cleaner streets. Both of these could potentially limit pickers' access to waste. The last point, 'support to market development' could conceivably benefit the pickers if it enabled them to sell their waste at higher prices. However, if the other policy changes were being put in place, then market support could only ever be a short-term, and hence a non-sustainable, measure because access to waste would be threatened in the longer term.

- ***DFID suggested intervention: Feedback from achievement of livelihood outcomes (virtuous cycles)*** *through a more sustainable use of natural resources leading to improvement of stocks of natural capital, and investment in natural capital leading to higher incomes.* This raises the issue of 'sustainable use of resources', which is difficult to conceptualise in terms of waste. It also suggests a 'positive correlation between higher income and investment in natural capital'. The very opposite is likely to be true; investment in natural capital for pickers would be likely to compromise their livelihoods and incomes by cleaning the streets and limiting their access to waste.

A number of issues emerge here. Firstly, it is clear that the nature and characteristics of pickers' natural capital are very different from those of a farmer, most notably with regard sustainability and the results of investment. Secondly, there may exist a tension between wider environmental and development interests (i.e. cleaner streets) and the livelihood interests of pickers. As such, natural capital related interventions for waste pickers need to be approached in fundamentally different ways from those applicable in rural areas.

3.3.2 Definitions and issues of sustainability

Definitions

A farmer's natural capital consists of land, water, soil, and forests etc. Defining natural capital for a waste picker however is less easy, but it could sensibly be considered 'valuable waste'. The sustainable livelihoods approach incorporates a detailed study of natural capital, but many of the suggested areas are not relevant to waste pickers or to the urban context in general. Some of the aspects that do not translate easily are as follows;

- Access rights. These were not considered an issue or problem by any picker interviewed.
- Land ownership. No land is required to pick waste, and most areas from which waste can be picked are communal.
- Conflict over resources. Not reported to be a problem by any participants, except in one instance where the boys in the Mirpur hostel described a situation where two pickers simultaneously saw a piece of valuable waste, and an argument ensued. This was not a frequent occurrence.
- Requirement for inputs. No inputs or effort are required to develop or sustain the production of waste.
- Sustainability issues. Waste is available freely and supplies renew themselves daily. The only realistic threat to the sustainability concern changes in the way waste is managed.

Certain aspects of natural capital apply in both the rural and urban setting as follows;

- Seasonality. It has been shown that seasonal variations in quantity and value and nature of waste do occur.
- Productivity. This concept could loosely be described as the value of waste. For waste pickers themselves, the waste itself 'produces' nothing other than income. In the wider context, waste collected produces recycled materials and products.
- Trends. While few trends have been found, it is likely that an overall increase in waste quantities has characterised the last decade, and that 'invisible trends' may exist.
- Spatial Variation. Spatial variation has been found to exist in the nature and availability of waste.

Sustainability

The very name of the 'sustainable livelihoods approach' suggests great emphasis on sustainability, and it is clearly important. However, improved conservancy aside, issues surrounding the sustainability of 'waste' as natural capital are unclear and depend on perspective.

In terms of pure supply and demand, waste use at present levels could justifiably be termed 'totally sustainable' as more is generated than 'harvested'. There is little risk of 'undermining the resource base'. However, another aspect of sustainability relates to the environment. Normally, environmental sustainability relies on resources being used sparingly. However, in the wider perspective of global resource use, the *more* waste collected by pickers (and hence recycled rather than dumped), the more resources are being used in an environmentally sustainable manner. In terms of definitions and drawing links between rural and urban concepts, these issues are important.

The nature of the sustainability of waste as a resource and of waste pickers' livelihoods may raise very different sustainability issues from those of rural areas. 'Sustainability' of natural resources as well as *access* to them are vital for the sustainability of all livelihoods.

3.3.3 Improved solid waste management

In rural areas, development interventions relating to natural capital are mostly designed to benefit farmers and the resources are considered desirable. For pickers, development interventions relating to what constitutes their natural capital can undermine their livelihoods, and the resource is considered highly undesirable. This highlights the fundamental differences between the natural resource base in the rural and this urban context. It also describes one of the threats that development can (and is likely to) pose to waste pickers. The livelihoods of waste pickers rely entirely on access to a continuous supply of solid waste, and to a great degree on its continued poor management by the authorities. In rural areas there is less of the tension between poverty and environmental developmental agendas which clearly exists in the urban setting for waste pickers.

The fictitious example in Box 2 describes the effect that improved solid waste management may have on a picker in Dhaka. Despite this example, it is difficult to justify resisting improvements to solid waste management, because the benefits are likely to far outweigh the disadvantages if only in utilitarian terms. This means however, that there is an anomaly. The study of waste pickers here, using the sustainable livelihoods approach, is ultimately aiming at enabling pickers to make their livelihoods more resilient and sustainable. However, SLA based interventions are (rightly so) intended to be holistically informed, multi-sectoral and to have identified and encompassed all the influencing forces. The approach cannot ignore (or discourage) interventions working towards better solid waste management in a city with such problems. Therefore, assuming such intervention will take place and that access to waste would be disrupted, the livelihoods of waste pickers *as they stand* cannot be viewed in any way as sustainable.

This means that the emphasis of livelihood work with waste pickers may have to involve encouraging fundamental changes in the nature of their livelihoods rather than trying to encourage them to make their existing livelihoods more sustainable. It may be only then that pickers would be able to withstand the inevitable shocks of improved conservancy. This is not, however, a hopeless conclusion to draw (and may be incorrect anyway). One suggestion as to how the interests of all stakeholders could be met, involving a subtle change in livelihood activities for pickers, is described below.

Box 2. Monir and the effects of improved conservancy

Monir has been waste picking for many years. Before coming to Dhaka he was a farmer. He thought that, while picking may be an unpleasant occupation, it was at least secure and predictable in comparison to farming. Waste was generated daily by the population and dumped throughout the city enabling pickers to harvest it at will. It could be harvested and sold all year and prices were not liable to large or unpredictable variations. There were no access problems and never any worry about resources running low; the supply was self-regenerating. In farming he had faced all of these worries.

Only one thing threatened the sustainability of his natural capital and hence the sustainability of his livelihood. This was improved solid waste management. Waste on the streets looks bad, smells bad and is a health hazard to the population at large. As a result, the municipal authorities, funded by numerous international NGOs, implemented an effective strategy to remove waste from the streets more efficiently.

The effects of this on Monir were that his access to waste decreased. Monir suffered a drop in income. As a result of this drop in income he needed to borrow money whilst trying to find alternative employment. However, the demise of his livelihood was accompanied by the demise of his primary financial coping mechanism; the relationship with his dealer. Livelihoods from picking were no longer secure, so the dealer was not willing to lend money. Monir faced difficult times.

3.3.4 Livelihood substitution: a possibility for intervention

It could be concluded that wider development objectives and the livelihoods of pickers are completely at odds. However, there are ways in which the needs of both groups could be met whilst realising both the environmental and poverty objectives.

It is possible that improved solid waste management could absorb the jobs lost by waste pickers as a result of the changes. This would involve a process called livelihood substitution. One such example of how this may be achieved is in the employment of pickers as door-to-door collectors. Door-to-door collectors collect waste directly from households for a small monthly fee. This means that waste is no longer deposited on the streets. The pickers (now 'collectors') continue to have access to the valuable waste for sorting and selling, but they no longer have to search for it in such unpleasant circumstances, and their status is likely to be raised. This livelihood substitution would mean that waste pickers also benefited from and participated in the improved solid waste management. In addition, their sorting and waste selling activities would continue, and so other important aspects of their livelihoods are preserved, such as their relationship with dealers.

This scheme is not mentioned or flagged as a panacea for waste pickers, and neither is it a new idea. Such schemes are operating throughout Bangladesh already, though most of these are small scale, and often NGO-initiated and run as microenterprises. Further research is required into the plans of the Dhaka City Corporation and other implementing agencies, and into the effects this would have on pickers. There are likely to be other examples of how livelihood substitution can take place, and of how the process of development can progress without severely disadvantaging certain stakeholders.

3.3.5 Summary

This section is not intended to demonstrate that the examination of natural capital is not relevant or useful to the study of livelihoods. It is intended to demonstrate the need to adapt this aspect of the sustainable livelihoods framework. Close examination of the nature of natural capital for waste pickers has highlighted a number of livelihood-threatening elements, most notably the threat of improved conservancy. Understanding these threats, and the nature of the natural capital for pickers, is essential for effective intervention.

3.4 Physical capital

DFID objective:
> *'Access to basic and facilitating infrastructure' (DFID 1999: 2.3.4)*

Waste pickers in Dhaka lack access to the basic infrastructure, and the limited access they do enjoy is often not realised because of prohibitively high costs. The components of infrastructure considered (by DFID) vital for a sustainable livelihood are secure shelter and buildings, clean affordable energy, adequate water supply and sanitation, access to information and affordable transport.

Little is known about pickers' need for or access to many aspects of infrastructure. Most information exists on the pickers' shelter and buildings, described below. Access to information is likely to be limited because the pickers are generally illiterate and sources of information, like their means of communication, may be restricted to within social networks. Information about waste prices, recycling, small loan facilities, education and health care could potentially aid pickers in their livelihood pursuits. Transport is not a requirement for pickers' work, but many are migrants from rural areas, and the need to return to visit family may arise. In such circumstances the cost of journeys is likely to be high when set against their salaries, though a number of pickers spoke of travelling on the roofs of trains for free.

The reasons for pickers' lack of access to infrastructure are discussed in Section 4, Transforming structures and processes.

3.4.1 Living conditions

The living conditions of many of the participants in this research demonstrate the lack of services available to them, as well as the lack of what constitutes 'good shelter' (DFID 1999). Of those pickers interviewed who have homes, all were situated in *bustees*. The buildings in these are generally constructed from a mixture of mud, iron sheeting and leaves. Some homes in slums have electricity, but the cost of this is not known, and the primary fuel for cooking is wood and leaves which is very smoky. A number of slum houses have wells in or near them,

Photograph 4. Raju and Jushim in the Begum Bari bustee

and in certain areas there is piped water. There is little or no sanitation or effective drainage in any of the slums visited. The *bustees* are crowded, lack privacy, and most are unplanned. Photograph 4 shows two participants, Raju and Jushim, outside their homes in their roadside *bustee* in Begum Bari.

The following information was collected from a variety of verbal sources, mostly other researchers who have worked in and studied the *bustees*. There can be a problem with collecting information about the *bustees* from pickers themselves. They may be hesitant to speak to researchers whom they suspect to be Government officials and hence present a threat to their homes.

If the information overleaf is an accurate representation of the situation in *bustees* then it is clear that a bottleneck exists in terms of services provision to inhabitants.

The objective of the SLA is to develop better access to facilitating infrastructure. A broader objective of the approach is sustainability, and because of the uncertainty of the future of the *bustees* and the land on which they stand, any intervention may be inherently temporary in nature. Careful research at government through to 'ground' levels would be required to determine what, if any, intervention could be sustainable. More detailed information on the power relations in *bustees* would also be vital in terms of deciding the nature of any

---

Box 3. Dhaka bustees

The land on which *bustees* in Dhaka are situated is generally owned by the Government, but the *bustees* are 'run' by landlords. The landlords are often Government officials themselves who collect ground rents from inhabitants. All services supplied to the homes, including electricity, water and gas, are controlled by them. Slum dwellers reputedly pay the landlords highly inflated prices for these services. There is usually a dearth of sanitation facilities, and some NGOs are working to improve them. The government is reluctant to provide sewerage systems for fear of legitimising the existence of the settlements.

In addition to the lack of services, there is also a constant insecurity regarding the future of the *bustees*. As Dhaka grows, so too does the need for land for construction. *Bustees* are owned by the government, and the landlords may sometimes be persuaded to relinquish the land by incentives greater than the sum of all ground rents.

---

intervention, and in deciding the level at which changes would need to be made. Short of moving all *bustee* dwellers elsewhere, it seems that fundamental changes at the government and *bustee* landlord levels would be required.

While most of the participants live in these slums, many pickers in Dhaka live rough on the streets (e.g. Muman) and others seek refuge in hostels for the homeless and underprivileged, such as Shafi in Mirpur. Muman and Shafi represent both ends of the spectrum in terms of the housing and services available to pickers.

3.5 Financial capital

DFID objective:
> *'More secure access to financial resources'. (DFID 1999: 2.3.5).*

One of the most striking differences between rural and urban areas is the cost of living. In rural areas water and fuel are likely to be cheaper or free, some food may be freely available (such as fruit) and if a person owns land they may have the means to survive by growing crops. In a city however, everything requires money. There is a shortage of land in Dhaka, and almost none for growing crops. There is very little communal land, and any free fruit is likely to have been stolen from people's gardens, or picked from the floor in markets[4]. Given the situation in *bustees,* water may be costly, and according to participants, fuel for cooking invariably has to be purchased.[5] As a result, financial capital is an essential resource of waste pickers in Dhaka.

Financial capital exists in three forms; income, savings, and credit.

3.5.1 Incomes

Considerable data was collected about incomes, and some has already been presented in the form of seasonal charts. Incomes are usually in the region of Tk40 to Tk200 (US$0.80 to $4.00) per day. Tk200 is an exceptional income, achieved only by Shahib Ali; the oldest male picker in the sample who worked up to 12 hours per day. According to pickers with families, most income is given to parents and a few Taka retained for buying sweets or some other treat. Pickers such as Muman who are independent often save a proportion of their incomes, while others, such as those in Mirpur, have to give a proportion of their earnings to pay for their keep in the hostel.

3.5.2 Savings

The facilities available, and the keenness of many pickers to save, were striking. Pickers were saving money for a variety of reasons. Muman was found to be saving daily with a local shopkeeper and claimed to have amassed Tk1000 (US$20), a considerable sum of money. He was saving in order that he had a contingency for periods of illness or other emergencies, but also because he intended to return to the village from which he came to farm family land with his siblings. Other boys were saving with hostels. The Mirpur hostel had a sophisticated savings scheme and actively encouraged the boys to save some of their earnings. Shafi had two savings funds with the hostel; one for short term emergencies (to pay his fees if he was ill or wanted some time off work), and one fund to which he could not gain immediate access, intended for his future.

Saving is an important coping mechanism for pickers. More information is needed about the facilities that enable them to save, including the reliability and social dynamics that characterise those in existence. Some of the pickers, particularly those who were helping to support impoverished families, were not able to save any money. These pickers (or their families) would have to turn to other sources for meeting their financial needs in times of emergency. Many would turn to family or friends, but others would need to borrow money.

3.5.3 Borrowing

The main source of credit for pickers is their dealers. This has already been discussed in Section 3.2.2 'Relationship with Dealers'. The reason for describing this financial resource there in preference to this section is because it constitutes a social asset, and only the result of the relationship is financial.

The service that dealers supply is vital for the continued availability of financial capital for waste pickers. This is important both for enabling pickers to survive through periods when they cannot work (e.g. due to illness), as well as for providing them with an opportunity to invest in themselves or in an alternative livelihood. Examples of these may include borrowing money to pay for training or to live on whilst training is taking place and normal livelihood activities cannot be pursued. In terms of alternative livelihoods, Jakeel Hussein, a dealer in the Korail *bustee* reports having lent money to some pickers to enable them to buy tricycles for door-to-door collection. The returns for Jakeel on such a loan would be high because the capacity of the picker to collect valuable waste would increase significantly with a tricycle, and Jakeel is guaranteed the collector's trade.

Jakeel was asked about the availability of other sources of credit. He said that there were no other sources, and no money lenders working in the *bustees*.

This provision of money for emergencies and training is very much in line with the livelihood priorities of DFID. The study of existing coping mechanisms and credit sources is likely to elicit valuable lessons and guidance for schemes to make such facilities accessible to more pickers, as well as clarifying the impacts of new schemes on existing services.

Figure 3. Asset pentagon

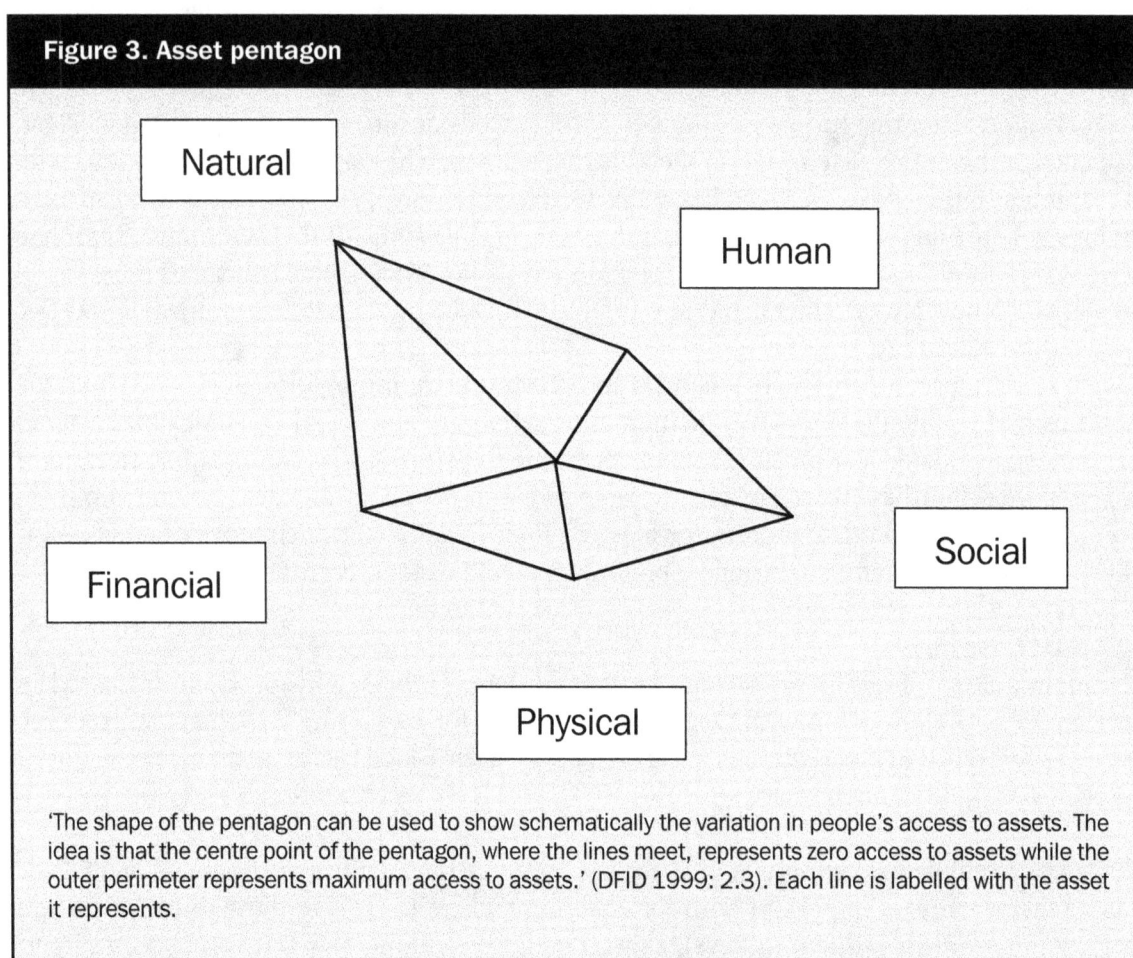

'The shape of the pentagon can be used to show schematically the variation in people's access to assets. The idea is that the centre point of the pentagon, where the lines meet, represents zero access to assets while the outer perimeter represents maximum access to assets.' (DFID 1999: 2.3). Each line is labelled with the asset it represents.

3.6 The asset pentagon

To attempt to draw an 'asset pentagon' indicating the relative strengths, availabilities and trends in pickers' assets is very difficult. This is, in part, on account of the difficulty in *quantifying* the assets, but also because there is significant 'overlap' between the various forms of capital.

The process of constructing an asset pentagon requires each asset to be quantified in terms of its availability, ease of access and value. This constitutes an overall impression of asset endowment. The pentagon can also include any trends that exist by the inclusion of arrows. A carefully constructed pentagon is capable of communicating a substantial amount of information about livelihoods, and could be a useful tool in distilling information into a model that can highlight areas of need. The careful construction of an asset pentagon is likely to be a time consuming process.

Figure 3 constitutes a *sketch* of an asset pentagon representing the asset profile of waste pickers in Dhaka. Insufficient data exists for an accurate pentagon to be drawn and this is based on an *overall impression* from field work findings. No attempt has been made to formally quantify or compare access rights, quantities or values of the individual assets and no trends have been included.

Natural capital (waste) is indicated as the greatest of pickers' assets, and physical the least. Social capital is stronger than human or financial.

4.
Transforming structures and processes

'The institutions, organisations, policies and legislation that shape livelihoods' (DFID 1999: 2.4).

This aspect of the SLA is an area for which there is a shortage of information. This is partly due to the emphasis of the research, but also the apparent general lack of interaction between waste pickers and the policies and structures which define and shape Dhaka.

4.1 Structures

'Structures...are the hardware...that set and implement policy and legislation, deliver services, purchase, ...and perform all manner of other functions that affect livelihoods.' *(DFID 1999: 2.4.1)*

Waste pickers appear to be marginalised in such a way that many of the structures that 'perform functions that affect livelihoods' are inaccessible to them. One such example involves the legal system. Access to a legal system at both street level (the police) and at higher levels (the judicial system) is an empowering asset, and can provide valuable protection to personal well being, rights and property. Pickers lack any such access. Many pickers fear the police, and would not be able to turn to them for help if in need. The reasons for this are complex, and associated with general stigmatisation and the frequent association of pickers with criminals. There are also reports of arrests that take place whereby pickers are made scapegoats for crimes they did not commit. One hostel[8] for street children working in the Farm Gate area described how many pickers and other street children were in custody having been arrested simply in order to achieve police arrest targets.

No pickers could think of any community organisations of which they were members and the *existence* of any such group was never referred to. There was some NGO activity but certain *bustee* dwellers commented that the 'microenterprise and credit organisations are all based in the rural areas'. NGO health clinics and education services do exist but they are inadequate.

4.2 Processes

'Processes can be thought of as software. They determine the way in which structures – and individuals – operate and interact.' These include policies, legislation, institutions, culture and power relations. (DFID 1999: 2.4.2)

The effects on waste pickers of two aspects of national policy and legislation have already been discussed in some detail. These are the effects of changes (i.e. improvements) in solid waste management (Section 3.3.3), and the effects of government decisions concerning use of land in Dhaka, notably the land on which the slums are sited (Section 3.4.1). These lead to changes in pickers' access to waste and threaten their homes respectively. However, in general, waste pickers' livelihoods seem to be strikingly insulated from higher level national policy and intervention. No picker could think of any way in which the authorities and legislation impacted their livelihood positively or negatively. There are no policies that affect their access to waste, which constitutes their main resource.

Too little is known of the culture in Bangladesh to describe ways in which it determines pickers' activities. However, picking is clearly considered a culturally low-status occupation, and as such pickers are often treated as low-status individuals. This is likely to account for some of their marginalised nature and isolation from society, as well as their stigmatisation. Various pickers described how they were considered by some to be thieves or criminals simply on account of their occupation.

There are also aspects of class, caste, religion and age which could be further investigated, not tackled in this research. Gender is discussed below.

4.2.1 Gender Issues

There are some gender issues for pickers, but because little of this research was carried out with females little is understood in any detail. Below is a description of an isolated experience which served to reveal attitudes towards a group of girls as pickers. It may or may not serve to represent general attitudes.

Box 4. Girls in the Korail *bustee*

In the Korail *bustee* some girls were returning mid-morning with sacks on their heads and appeared to have been out waste picking. It transpired they had been picking leaves only and not waste (leaves are collected for burning and cooking). When asked why they did not collect any waste they said 'Our parents do not wish us to pick waste as they fear it would make us become thieves.'

It may be that the nuance of what they said was lost in translation, and that in fact their parents were concerned that their daughters would *appear* to be thieves. However, this serves to confirm the existence of negative attitudes in general towards waste pickers, even amongst other *bustee* inhabitants.

The fact that little research was undertaken with girls is an important gender issue in itself. This was partly due to there being more male pickers than females, but also because both researchers were male. Given the prevailing cultural norms in Bangladesh, there are difficulties associated with interviewing female pickers, and they were not nearly as keen to offer their participation as boys. More work would need to be done on this area, and it is possible (though not known for sure) that female researchers would be required to facilitate work with girls and women.

4.3 Access to infrastructure

According to research findings, waste pickers appear to be very marginalised, and little of the country's infrastructure & legislation appears to have an effect on them. Reasons for their lack of access and influence may include the following;

- legal barriers (e.g. laws prohibiting their involvement);
- physical barriers (e.g. distance);
- cultural barriers (e.g. cultural norms);
- educational barriers (e.g. requirement for literacy);
- knowledge barriers (e.g. they just do not know about it); or,
- cost barriers (i.e. prohibitive cost).

As with the case of physical capital, more questions need to be asked, and answered through research, about why access to infrastructure is so poor, why it needs to be improved and how better access can be achieved.

5.
Livelihood strategies

DFID livelihood objective:
> *'To promote choice, opportunity and diversity' (DFID 1999: 2.5).*

This is a valuable aspect of livelihoods to examine as it reveals reasoning behind present livelihood activities and the options and alternatives available.

Waste picking is frequently the first livelihood activity undertaken by a new arrival to Dhaka. It is popular in this respect because it requires little knowledge, few skills and no capital (no purchase of tools / equipment is necessary). However, many pickers continue picking for many years after their arrival, such as Shafi and Muman. They both arrived alone as young boys, began picking immediately and have been picking ever since. Waste picking is not solely an occupation of new arrivals.

Other aspects of livelihood strategies have been discussed in the 'Seasonality' and 'Financial capital' sections with regard to forward planning and contingencies. The ability of very young pickers to consider the future and strategise their livelihood is remarkable, though the facilities to enable them to save money are not sufficiently widespread.

5.1 Livelihood 'straddling'

Livelihood straddling is a strategy found to be pursued by a number of the pickers interviewed. This describes a situation wherein a given picker undertakes two or more livelihood activities. Saddam claimed to undertake many paid activities when not picking including rickshaw repair, singing and dancing, being a messenger and begging. Shahib Ali, supporting himself and his mother, worked in a dealer's shop in the evenings after having finished picking. Of the focus group participants, three boys in Mirpur sold ice cream during the hot season in addition to picking. From the Korail *bustee* group, three boys said they sold sweet potatoes when they were in season during March.

5.2 Livelihood alternatives

Some pickers feel they have no alternative to picking and are effectively trapped in their present livelihood. One such example is Shahib Ali, who on account of being innumerate, does not consider himself capable of other work. It seems that for some pickers there may be a genuine lack of choice in whether or not to continue picking.

Livelihood alternatives that exist for pickers mostly include activities that require minimal capital input, little training and few skills. These include rickshaw driving, delivering messages, entertaining, begging and door to door waste collection. Some boys also mentioned the possibility of future employment with Dhaka City Corporation as part of the city conservancy team.

Training opportunities in the weaving and garments industry were discussed in Section 3.1.3. It described how, although alternative occupations exist, the opportunity cost of the required training was prohibitively high. This is an important factor in understanding options for waste pickers with very few reserves and contingencies to facilitate changes in circumstance. Section 3.1.3 concluded that pickers required ways of enabling them to sustain themselves and their families through periods of low income experienced as a result of training for jobs which ultimately pay more.

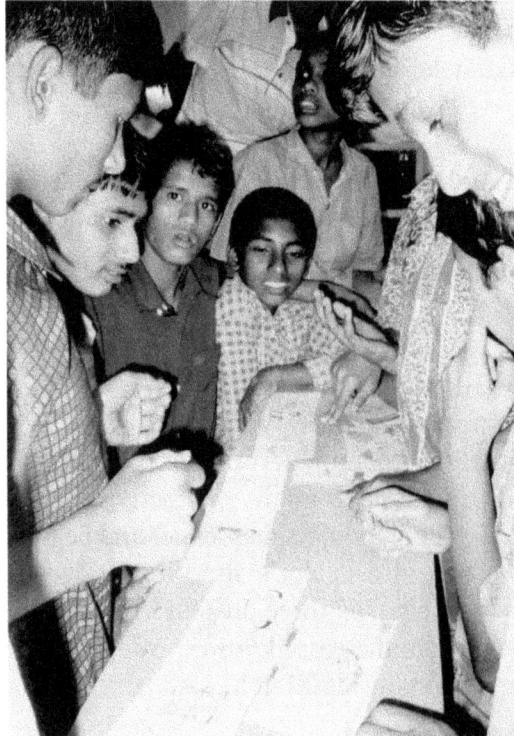

Photograph 5. Mirpur boys arranging ranking cards

6.
Livelihood outcomes

DFID livelihood objective (summary):

To identify the livelihood outcomes that pickers themselves pursue, and the factors preventing these goals from being realised. (DFID 1999: 2.6)

The examination of livelihood outcomes enables a comparison between *actual* livelihood outcomes and people's *aspirations* for their livelihood outcomes. Livelihood outcomes are described as 'the achievements and outputs of Livelihood Strategies.' (DFID 1999: 2.6). It is important to recognise that pickers' priorities for livelihood outcomes may not be obvious, or match a researcher's expectations. For example, pickers may value having company during picking more than having a higher income.

It is vital to understand the priorities, objectives and ambitions of pickers in order to facilitate the effective design of interventions that address pickers' specific needs as well as broader development objectives. The following section describes the ranking exercise in which participants in the two focus groups expressed the different value they attached to different aspects of their lives.

6.1 Focus group ranking exercise

Participants in the two focus groups were asked to rank various aspects of their lives in order of the importance they attached to them. Photograph 5 opposite, shows the boys at Mirpur gathered round the cards discussing the order in which they should be arranged.

6.1.1 Results

The results of their ranking are shown in Table 3. These give a valuable insight into the priorities and aspirations of the participants. They also reveal marked differences between the two groups, which may reflect the different circumstances of the participants, and the way in which they view their circumstances. The differences also reaffirm the need to recognise that

Table 3. Ranking exercise results		
Mirpur focus group	**Korail focus group**	
1. Enough food	1. Having a job	Most important
2. Freedom	2. Enough money	▲
3. A good house	3. Lots of money	
4. Education	4. A good house	
5. Good health	5. Family	
6. Secure house	6. Secure house	
7. Family	7. Enough good food	
8. Good clothes	8. Good clothes	
9. Having a job	9. Good health	
10. Money	10. Education	
11. Good friends	11. Good friends	
12. Being part of a group	12. Recreation	
13. Recreation	13. Group membership	▼
	14. Freedom	Least important

An additional card was introduced to the set for the Korail focus group, to enable participants to distinguish between 'lots of money' (i.e. being rich) and 'enough money'. See Part II Section 3.2.3 for more details.

waste pickers are not a single consistent group but a diverse set of people with different priorities and, as previously shown, different livelihood strategies.

When the Mirpur focus group had finished arranging the cards they were asked about the relative position of certain cards. This exercise was carried out at the end of the 1½ hour focus group, and the concentration of the boys was waning. This accounts for the limited discussion, and the lack of any discussion with the less disciplined and patient Korail *bustee* participants.

The boys were asked why they considered housing more important than having good friends. They said that in order to have friends it is necessary to have somewhere to entertain them. When asked why they also considered good clothes more important than friends they explained that they felt they are judged by friends according to the types of clothes they wear. This indicated that clothes are considered a status symbol, and further discussion revealed that the children might actually have been describing wearing *clean*, rather than 'good' (i.e. fashionable or expensive) clothes. Finally, the boys were asked why they had put money at the bottom of the list. They reconsidered the position of the money card, and put it to where it is shown in Table 3. One boy commented 'Why do we need money when all we need is enough to eat?'

6.1.2 Comparison of group results

There is considerable potential in the interpretation of these results, but in order to further demonstrate the potential use of this exercise just two examples of comparison will be described.

- **Freedom.** The position of this card may reflect the relative situations of the two groups. The Mirpur boys are in a hostel; an institution that inflicts many rules and restrictions on their movements. In contrast, the Korail group enjoys almost total freedom in its bustee situation. It is interesting to note the positions that Freedom was placed in terms of relative priorities. The Mirpur group rated it highly while the Korail group rated it least important, perhaps because it was simply not an issue for them.

- **Good clothes.** It was surprising to see that the Korail group considered having 'good clothes' more important than good health. When asked if they could explain this, one boy said that dirty clothes made them ill, and so clean clothes were a pre-requisite for good health. This provides an insight into a health issue which is also likely to relate to their work. It also highlights the importance of understanding the subtleties of participants' understanding of the cards and the ranking exercise itself. 'Good clothes' (indicated by a pair of jeans, shirt and leather sandals) was intended to mean good quality or smart clothes, but for the Korail children instinctively indicated clean clothes. In addition, the 'order of requirement' (e.g. good clothes are a pre-requisite of good health) is quite different from 'order of importance' (e.g. good clothes are more important than good health).

Accusations of 'jumping to conclusions with too little data' could be justifiably made about these examples, but they do not attempt to present 'facts', simply to demonstrate how data from such an exercise may be used and interpreted.

7.

The sustainable livelihoods approach as a tool

This section consolidates some of the conclusions reached by this research, with specific reference to the criteria stated in Section 1.3. These criteria, for assessing the merits and weaknesses of the SLA as a tool for studying and helping urban waste pickers' livelihoods, were as follows.

The sustainable livelihoods approach:

- How incisive?
- How relevant?
- How appropriate?
- How comprehensive?

These are examined and discussed below.

7.1 How incisive?

It is important to recognise that the sustainable livelihoods approach is a tool, and as such requires a skilled user. The SLA provides a framework that has been shown to be highly relevant in its basic structure for understanding the lives and livelihoods of waste pickers. However, the way in which it is used determines its incisiveness as much as its content, and skill of the user determines the extent to which it tackles and explores the more subtle and 'concealed' dynamics of livelihoods.

A carefully considered methodology is vital, and the integrity to know when to adapt or even ignore aspects of the framework is an important part in determining its effectiveness. The methodology employed in this study had clear weaknesses from which lessons and guidance for future research can and should be drawn.

7.2 How relevant?

The main issues that have become apparent with regards relevance concern rural to urban transitions. The SLA provides a useful and potentially incisive framework for studying livelihoods, but it is necessary to adapt certain parts of it in order to make them relevant to pickers.

Most aspects of the framework that do not transpose well to the urban setting are problematic only in terminology, and the *concepts* that underlie them are highly relevant. Seasonality is one area that has been shown to present 'difficulties' with reference to waste and pickers' livelihoods. Another is in the definition natural capital itself, and the fundamentally different methods of addressing natural capital of farmers and that of pickers (i.e. waste). Principles remain highly relevant; understanding aspects of sustainability and the characteristics of natural capital for pickers is a vital part of understanding livelihoods.

One area in which many of the concepts do not apply strongly to pickers is covered by 'Physical Capital' and 'Transforming Structures and Processes'. Amongst other things, these aspects of the SLA pose questions about 'macro-micro interlinkages' and the interaction between pickers and national infrastructure. These are based on the premise that such interlinkages and interaction exist, whereas this research indicates (albeit inconclusively) that few such relationships exist, and that pickers are largely insulated from such 'high level' influences.

7.3 How appropriate?

Certain issues of appropriateness are very similar to those of relevance relating to the adaptation of rural to urban concepts. In addition to these, there are 'appropriateness issues' relating to the complexity of the concepts in the SLA.

Some of the concepts involved in SLA-based research are very complex. Section 3 of Part II discusses the way in which participants in research may find certain concepts difficult to understand or may have difficulty in articulating their responses. It is vital that concepts are presented to pickers in an appropriate way, as well as providing ways of expressing views or indicating preferences and trends in a way appropriate to their level of literacy and their outlook.

Appropriateness is not an issue for the SLA itself, but can become an issue if great care is not given to research techniques and methodology.

7.4 How comprehensive?

The SLA boasts an holistic consideration of factors affecting livelihoods. On the whole it was found that the SLA does provide a comprehensive and holistic framework for studying waste pickers' livelihoods. In the course of applying the underlying concepts of the SLA in this research, no areas of livelihoods came to light that were not covered by some part of the framework.

The comprehensive nature of the SLA could be in part because it looks carefully at interlinkages between different aspects, but also perhaps because many parts of it overlap. This is not a criticism of the approach. In fact the only point at which this presented problems was at the reporting stage, and it is perhaps a worthy lesson to note that attempting to describe a livelihood in a format based on the structure of the DFID SLA itself can be clumsy, as so many aspects of one section involve aspects of another. Some such examples involve links between Physical Capital and Transforming Processes and Structures, and Vulnerability context, Social Capital and Financial Capital.

Of course, the value of thoroughness far outweighs any difficulties that such an approach may impose on reporting, and appears to provide a comprehensive framework for understanding the dynamics of waste pickers' lives and livelihoods. The framework can be used (and was used) to good effect as the basis of a list of essential topics to be covered in the process of constructing a picture of livelihoods.

8.
Conclusion

This conclusion is divided into two sections, the first relating to the performance of the SLA, and the second to the livelihoods of waste pickers.

8.1 The sustainable livelihoods approach

The SLA successfully combines social, economic, institutional and physical aspects in an analysis that seemingly covers everything. However, in the course of the research in Dhaka it was found that there were certain parts of the SLA which were not relevant in the urban context, or which were inappropriate to the specific study of waste pickers. In addition, there was found to be considerable overlap between different parts of the framework. These factors meant that the SLA could not be used as an exact template for research, and that it was not adhered to dogmatically. Instead, the ideas and philosophy behind the approach formed the core of the research at design and implementation stages.

The following is taken from the DFID Sustainable Livelihoods Guidance sheets, and states exactly what was concluded from this study in Dhaka.

> 'A more important task than perfecting the framework itself is putting the ideas that it represents into practice. *If that calls for adaptation of certain boxes or revision of certain definitions to make the framework more useful, all the better; the framework becomes a living tool.*' (DFID 1999: 2.1. Author's italics)

The following two examples describe parts of the SLA which are not immediately relevant to urban waste pickers and require adaptation.

- *Natural capital* and related issues of sustainability. The concepts of generating and 'harvesting' waste (the natural capital of a picker) are very different from those for a farmer. Whereas the natural capital in a rural setting can easily be used in an unsustainable manner, it is difficult to conceptualise unsustainable use of waste by pickers. Despite fundamental differences, the examination of natural capital constituted a very valuable part of

47

the livelihood research, and highlighted some important short and long-term vulnerability issues.

- **Seasonal effects** on waste pickers' livelihoods are very different from those on a rural farmer, but understanding them is equally important. Waste pickers were found to be affected by the seasons and this impacted their ability to make their living, as well as their general well being.

The SLA is a tool and its employment requires skill, ingenuity and adaptability. Whether or not any of the specific aspects of the SLA are directly employed in studying urban waste pickers' livelihoods, the most valuable fundamental idea from it that could be put into practice is its holistic approach. This is key in understanding the complex interaction of issues relating to any livelihood.

8.2 The livelihoods of waste pickers

This research showed that the waste pickers consulted are marginalised from numerous aspects of society in Dhaka. They are not integrated into the formal financial system, have little access to the legal, health and education systems and many do not enjoy municipal services such as electricity, clean water and sanitation. Pickers are seen and treated by many as criminals and lower-class citizens and appear to hold a low status in society.

The research highlighted some of the many factors which make pickers' livelihoods fragile and vulnerable, including the seasons and dangers associated with their work and living conditions. It has shown how their livelihoods could be threatened by improved city conservancy and the associated long-term sustainability issues of their natural capital, (i.e. waste). This served to illustrate the tension that can exist between the environmental and poverty agendas in development, and the importance of endeavouring to integrate the two. In addition to livelihoods-related data, other aspects of the lives of pickers have been shown to be insecure, including their homes, the land on which they live and even their freedom.

Many waste pickers were found to be extremely resourceful individuals. All pickers consulted had a good knowledge of where to find particular types of waste. Many planned their activities according to value and quantity of waste, the weather, friends' work and the relative safety of different areas. Some pickers planned the financial side of their livelihoods strategically and saved money for a contingency fund or specific future enterprises.

Providing waste remains available and accessible, waste picking is an activity that can provide a steady and reliable income for as long as a picker is healthy. Many pickers, however, do not like their work, but there are clearly obstacles to their getting trained or moving into other areas of more attractive, better paid, work. One such obstacle is the opportunity cost of time spent training. Reducing this by providing loans or training suited to the working hours of pickers could enable pickers to have more choice in livelihoods pursuits.

A small sample of waste pickers was consulted in the course of this research, so few meaningful conclusions can be drawn from the findings. Much of the information provided by pickers was contradicted by others, and numerous discrepancies existed in findings about specific aspects of livelihoods, such as the nature of seasonal influences. In spite of this, certain conclusions can be drawn, particularly relating to the marginalised nature and vulnerability of pickers.

Finally, this investigation has served to highlight the need for, and potential use of further SLA-based research for assisting waste pickers. Certain specific areas for attention in future research are outlined in the next section.

9.
Future research scope

The work in Dhaka has identified four areas of valuable future research, described below.

- Research into the way in which gender, age, class, background, caste and religion affect and dictate livelihood activities, preferences and strategies. The power relations and social makeup of the *bustees* and communities in which pickers live could also be examined with regard their impact on social, physical and financial capital and livelihood strategies.

- Research into the future of solid waste management in Dhaka, and the ways in which waste pickers could be integrated into, and benefit from, changes. Further research could also be undertaken into how the informal support structures and social networks etc. of waste pickers may be affected by changes in conservancy or occupation.

- Research into trends in the composition of, and international trade in, solid waste. Research would look at the effect of these trends on the livelihoods of waste pickers. The composition of waste is tending towards becoming less organic and more 'valuable' and recyclable. The effect of this on waste pickers' livelihoods could be examined, alongside responses in the collection system and recycling industry. International trade could serve to reduce the value of the lower grade recyclables found on the streets by pickers.

- Research into strategies which reduce the extent to which waste pickers are marginalised, by making *processes* and *structures* more inclusive. The lack of interaction between pickers and national infrastructure and institutions has been illustrated in this booklet. It would be valuable to identify ways in which changes could be made at different levels to reduce the gap in service accessibility and provision between different groups in Dhaka.

Much of the above research topics would apply as much to the 'poorest of the poor' in general as to waste pickers specifically.

Part II: Field Notes

Outline

The purpose of this part of the booklet is to present the field notes and lessons learned from the research. It attempts to discuss some of the issues that need to be understood when working closely with the poor.

The first section provides some background information about the research and describes some of the methodology used in the fieldwork. The second section focuses on the people for whom this research was carried out, highlighting issues relating to choice of research participant and listening to those in most need.

Section 3 describes and discusses some of the problems associated with communication between the researcher and the researched. The importance of recognising misunderstandings and ambiguity in fieldwork, and the existence of different perspectives is illustrated with examples. A number of the methods used to enable and encourage clarity of expression, on the parts of the researcher as well as participants, are also described.

Section 4 outlines a number of general issues relating to the fieldwork and suggests ways in which their negative effects can be minimised. The final section provides a summary of the Field Notes section.

1.
Fieldwork methodology

1.1 The researcher and local collaborators

The fieldwork was undertaken by one Englishman (the principle author) with the assistance of Mr Hasnat Iftekhar Hossain, a Bangladeshi who worked as a translator and field assistant. Assistance was also provided by a second Bangladeshi, Mr Shafiul Azam, who was present for some of the fieldwork and planning. Mr Azam worked for the Water and Sanitation Programme, Bangladesh (WSP) in Dhaka. These two people provided invaluable insights into the area and research topic which would have been extremely difficult to obtain through non-local contacts.

Local collaboration is considered by many to be a pre-requisite of overseas research ventures. However, it seems important to ask where priorities lie in seeking collaboration. Are they in 'local' or in *genuine* 'collaboration'? Local researchers can offer an unmatchable depth of knowledge and insight in various areas through fluency in local languages/dialects and intimate understanding of local culture and practices. However, if a local collaborator does not understand and share the outlooks and methodological approach of a researcher, the value of local knowledge may be limited. The same could be said of understanding and being sympathetic towards the objectives and ethics that underpin the research. In situations where a local collaborator with similar outlook cannot be found, it may be that a similarly minded foreign collaborator would, overall, be more valuable.

Much of the research in Dhaka was participatory in nature, and required a translator who understood the philosophy of open ended, open-*minded* research techniques. Hasnat Iftekhar was conversant with concepts of open-ended discussion and questioning and participatory group-work. This was essential for effective research and enabled a good partnership in fieldwork. Despite this, on occasion loaded questions were being asked and participants were being guided towards providing information that Iftekhar had come to know was 'required'. This was due to subtle misunderstandings in the reason behind asking certain questions, as well as perhaps a deeper misunderstanding of the desire to be *given* information rather than to 'take' or infer it.

Iftekhar was not primarily a translator but a field-researcher who was able to translate. He has undertaken research with children in the past and already had a good knowledge of waste pickers and their work. This latter experience was very useful and means that it is possible that he will use, or continue, this research in the future. This is an obvious longer-term benefit of employing individuals with genuine interest and involvement in the work after a given piece of research finishes. This was also the case with Mr Azam of the Water and Sanitation Programme, Bangladesh who is involved in solid waste research.

1.2 Time and duration of fieldwork

The fieldwork for this booklet was undertaken over a period of two months from March 2000. There was no specific reason for having chosen this time. This was the dry season in Dhaka when temperatures were highest, at up to 40^{0}C. It was not the most uncomfortable period of the year, which falls at the beginning of the monsoon when the high temperatures combine with up to 100 percent humidity.

In the course of this field work the effects of the seasons were studied in some detail. At the time of research, it was clear that heat was a limiting factor for the pickers. This was mentioned by some of the pickers, but it was also clear to the fieldworkers who were experiencing the intense heat and exaggerated stench of decomposing waste first-hand. Given the value of first-hand observation and experience by fieldworkers during research, it may be that conducting the research at different points in the year would give greater insight into the effect of climate on the pickers.

1.3 Initial observations

Before formal research began it was important for the researchers to orientate themselves in Dhaka. This enabled them to understand where the pickers lived and worked and to select a variety of contrasting areas in which to conduct research.

Research was undertaken using a variety of participatory techniques with both individuals and groups. Methodologies are outlined, in turn, below.

1.4 Research with individuals

Nine individual informants were interviewed for this research. They were located in five contrasting areas of Dhaka as indicated in Table 4.

These areas were chosen to enable comparison of a range of waste pickers' livelihoods in Dhaka. It was also anticipated that study of different types of areas could reveal trends in the spatial variation of waste in Dhaka and its impact on livelihoods. The pickers tended to work in areas away from their homes, mostly because they came from very poor areas and the waste in wealthier areas is likely to be more valuable.

Table 4. Research areas for individual participants	
Area/place name	**Characterised by**
Banani	**High income** inhabitants
Mirpur	**Low income** inhabitants
Begum Bari	**Industry** & low income inhabitants
Matuail	Solid waste municipal **landfill site**
Farm Gate	Numerous '**street children**'

NB. 'High income' and 'Low income' are not quantitative terms but are based on common knowledge of the areas and observation of type and quality of housing.

Table 5. Details of individual participants			
Name	**Location**	**Sex**	**Age***
Nasir	Korail bustee	M	~ 15
Saddam	Korail bustee	M	~ 7
Shahib Ali	Mirpur hostel	M	~ 25
Shafi	Mirpur hostel	M	14
Maleka	Matuail dump	F	34
Jussna	Matuail dump	F	~ 9
Raju	Begum Bari	M	~ 14
Jushim	Begum Bari	M	~ 9
Muman	Farm Gate	M	~ 12

* Most participants were unsure of their exact age. Uncertainty is indicated by '~'.

The names and details of the individual participants in this research are provided above in Table 5.

When points of particular interest and relevance to individual participants are cited, they are referenced using their name as given above.

Photograph 6. Fieldwork in Banani

Waste pickers are easily located in Dhaka. In general, the researchers would arrive at a slum or an area known to be inhabited by pickers early in the morning (usually at around 7am) and locate potentially suitable candidates. After brief introductions and explanations, providing the pickers felt comfortable, two researchers would join them for a few hours observing and discussing their work. Interviews were carried out 'on the move' for three reasons. The first was to avoid the inevitable accumulation of a crowd (by keeping moving this was less of a problem). Secondly, it provided an insight into the activities of the pickers in their work as researchers were with them during a relatively normal day. The third reason was that any time a picker spends not working can directly result in lost income. Income is proportional to the amount of waste collected.

None of the 'interviews' comprised solely of a set of questions. The facilitators had a set of issues in their minds, and would steer the conversation around these. Depending on how talkative or articulate the pickers were, issues that they themselves mentioned would also be explored and discussed. To gain information on all aspects of a picker's livelihood would require much time and effort and it was important to appreciate that these pickers were giving up time, and hence potential earnings, in talking to us. Hence, the objective was not to cover all livelihood issues with each individual, but to cover most issues with a range of individuals. Where information and understanding was lacking on certain aspect of livelihoods, conversation would be encouraged on that issue in the next meeting. Where possible a photograph was given to the participants at a later date as a token of thanks for their time and help. No payment was ever rendered.

1.5 Research using focus groups

A focus group is a meeting of a group of individuals used as a forum for discussing issues common to each participant. It is likely that a group of individuals will reveal different livelihood information from interviews with each member individually. A number of factors account for this such as the difference between being in a secure, familiar environment in the company of friends, and being in the sole company of an adult translator and a foreigner in a street. Participants in a group are also accountable to one another, and in group activities one individual is likely to be challenged if he or she makes a statement with which others disagree. Recording such disagreements can be valuable in themselves, whether resolved or not (Folch-Lyon, *et al.* 1981).

The focus group activities in this research were designed with children in mind and lessons from the first were embraced in the second. The use of pictures (latterly in the total absence of any written word) made the sessions accessible to all and entertaining for participants and facilitators alike. Entertainment held the participants' attention, and humour served to relax them. The use of pictures and tangible indicators (beans and picture-counters) also meant that there was a way of communicating ideas without the need for language.

Participants for the focus groups were chosen from two areas where research with individuals had already been undertaken. This meant that a relationship already existed with some of the group members, and that the facilitators were not completely new to the context. This made the meetings more relaxed due to the familiarity that existed from the outset, as well as easier to organise from a logistical viewpoint. The results were groups of pickers not of the same age or sex but of similar *circumstances*. Circumstances were found to be more likely to determine picking habits than age.

The areas chosen were quite different from one another, as described in Table 6.

Two activities were carried out in each focus group. The first was the completion of a seasonal chart, and the second a ranking exercise. The proceedings of the meetings are discussed in Section 3.2, Articulation and group work.

Table 6. Focus group areas	
Place/region name	**Characterised by**
Mirpur Boys' Hostel	A hostel for underpriviledged boys formerly living on the streets or abandoned in the slums, run by the joint Swiss – Bangladesh NGO Aparajeyo. It provides security, shelter, accommodation, health care and education for 50 boys. All the boys work, many as waste pickers, and pay Tk4 (US$0.08) per day to the hostel. Most of the boys are semi-literate. A boy called Shafi was previously known from hostel visits and had participated in the individual work. The Focus Group took place in the hostel building around a low table.
Korail Bustee	A slum south of Banani situated on government land. Like most slums in Dhaka its future is uncertain and it is 'run' by corrupt landlords and considered an insecure place. The boys and girls who participated in the focus group here were clearly very poor. They had received little or no formal education and were illiterate. The link with this slum was through Nasir who had participated in individual fieldwork. The Focus Group took place in a school classroom during the lunch break. The school is in the Korail Bustee and is run by 'Proshika', a Bangladeshi NGO. It was a simple tin building with matting floors and no furniture.

Photograph 7. Participants from the Korail focus group.

2.
Whose research and whose agenda?

2.1 Listening to 'quiet voices'

In the course of field work it became clear that there was a broad spectrum of pickers on the streets. Some boys were very personable, articulate, and loquacious and had lots of initiative and ambitious plans for the future. By contrast, other participants said very little, would not hold eye contact with researchers, had few opinions and/or were unable to express them well and had few hopes or ambitions for the future. The following are two examples of such contrasting pickers encountered during fieldwork.

Box 5. Contrasting personalities: Saddam and Shahib Ali

Saddam was a very gregarious seven year old boy from the Korail Bustee who was clearly very intelligent and had a lot of initiative. He was also very popular and in moving through the slum area people shouted his nickname 'Dollar' (Saddam proudly explained that he had acquired this nickname on account of his successful begging exploits at Dhaka international airport). Saddam had many ambitious ideas about the future, and intended to become an auto-rickshaw driver. He had attended school for some time and was keen to continue it at some point in the future. He did not intend to continue picking for very long.

Shahib Ali, who at 27 years of age was the oldest male participant in the research, seemed very uncomfortable with our presence. He appeared to be ill at ease in conversation. It transpired that he had suffered from mental illness (not defined) as a boy. He has now recovered following medical treatment for which he had to borrow money. As a result of his health he had not been to school. He said 'I will continue picking for ever. I won't get other work because I can't even count'.

The following example is based on the actual experience of gathering information from these two pickers. It illustrates how the personality of a picker will impact the nature, quality and quantity of information acquired. Saddam and Shahib Ali are chosen because they represent two furthest extremes amongst the participants.

Box 6. Who are we listening to?

Saddam. Saddam was very talkative and as a result, many pages of information were gathered about him and his livelihood. With little prompting he happily stopped to talk in depth about certain issues. Saddam enjoyed the attention. His picking success does not determine his survival; his earnings simply help the family out and provide him with a few *Taka* per day to buy some sweets. He was chosen from amongst the other boys because he had one of the loudest voices. The research morning was a pleasure and Saddam kept the researchers amused with his jokes, games and personality.

Shahib Ali. Shahib was not talkative and often did not (possibly could not) answer questions at all. He rarely said anything beyond the direct scope of questions. Shahib relies on his picking income to pay ground rent on his hut in a *bustee* and to buy food for himself and his widowed mother. As a result he was not willing to stop work to answer questions for any length of time, and during the brief stops his mind was clearly on his work, not the research. Shahib was not very friendly. Speaking to him and trying to find out about him exhausted the researchers.

Findings. The researchers found interviewing and gathering information about Saddam very much easier (and more enjoyable) than Shahib. They managed to compile a detailed and comprehensive 'Livelihood Profile' on Saddam. Information about Shahib, however, was scant and the researcher was left unconvinced that questions and issues being discussed were even understood because he was so unresponsive in his replies.

There are two important questions to ask at this point. 'Who is the research for?' and 'Who is the research about?' The answers to these questions *should* be the same. Unfortunately in the above example they are likely to be different. While information about Saddam is valuable, details about the life and livelihood of Shahib are in many ways more important. Saddam's survival does not depend on picking while Shahib and his Mother's survival do. Saddam is likely to stop picking soon, but Shahib is 'stuck' and set to continue picking into the foreseeable future. It is Shahib who is most in need of help from future intervention, but it is Saddam whose voice is most likely to be heard. This example illustrates the danger that reporting (and hence intervention) is based on research findings that are more about pickers like Saddam than Shahib, and hence not necessarily based on information from longer-term stakeholders and beneficiaries.

It is clearly vital to avoid the situation where the pickers who are being listened to most are those who are least likely to spend much of their working lives picking. As the above example shows, it is easy for this to happen. It is vital to build into future research ways of ensuring less articulate pickers, who may be less willing and able to participate, are heard and listened to.

2.2 A note on gender

There are certain gender issues for pickers, but because little of this research was carried out with females little is understood in any detail.

The fact that little research was undertaken with girls is an important gender issue in itself. This was partly due to there being more male pickers than females, but also because both researchers were male. Given the pervading cultural norms in Bangladesh, there are difficulties associated with males interviewing female pickers, and they were much less keen to offer their participation than boys. More work would need to be done on this area, and it is possible (although not known for certain) that female researchers would be required to facilitate work with girls and women.

3.
Communication

3.1 Language difficulties

One of the most notable limitations to effective research was language problems. All conversations and communication between participants and researcher in this study had to be conducted through a translator. This is likely to have resulted in valuable information not being recorded, and in inaccuracies in that which was recorded. This is not to say that the research was not useful or of value. However, as with any research, the ideal is where the recorder, interpreter and reporter of the information speak the same language as those with whom (and *for* whom) the research is being conducted.

3.2 Articulation and group work

Even without the language difficulties posed by a translated meeting, an individual may not have ever spoken about issues in the way in which he or she is being asked to by a researcher. This raises questions about the nature of the research topics (their complexity) as well as the appropriateness of the research techniques. Like uncovering 'invisible trends', this requires careful thought and incisive methodology. Methods of enabling people to express themselves need to be carefully prepared.

3.2.1 Focus groups

The focus group activities are examples of ways in which participants could express themselves without even using words (hence eliminating language problems). They are also examples of how it is possible to ask questions such as 'What trends exist in the annual cycle?' and 'What are the most and least important things in your life?' in an 'accessible' way whilst trying to minimise suggestion and 'loading' of questions.

Two main activities were carried out in the groups: the completion of a seasonal chart and a ranking exercise designed to reveal the priorities of pickers.

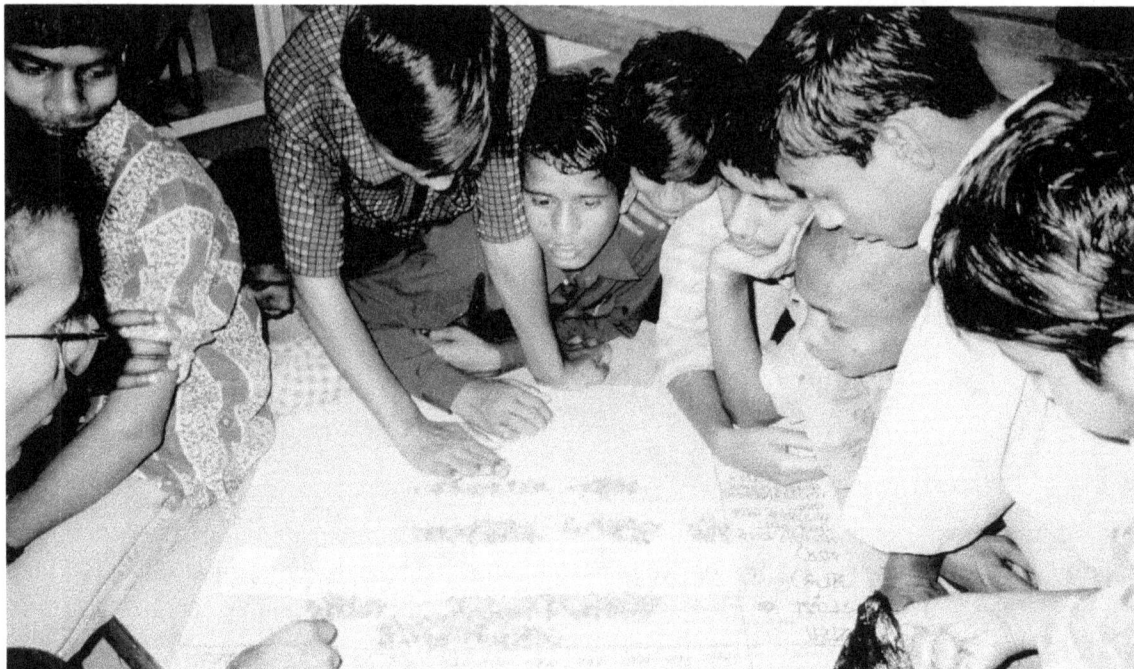

Photograph 8. The completion of the Mirpur group seasonal chart

3.2.2 Seasonal charts

The children were asked to indicate how a number of aspects of climate, life and livelihood varied throughout the year on a large seasonal chart. For the (semi-literate) Mirpur Group these aspects were labelled with pictures and Bangla words. Trends in these were marked under the twelve months of the year (in English) using dried peas, except for the 'Health' and 'Food and Nutrition' trends which were indicated by pictures on small squares of cards. Photograph 8 shows the chart as it was being completed by the boys at Mirpur.

The chart was made considerably simpler for the Korail *bustee* group as they were all illiterate. The year was split into three seasons (Hot and Dry, Hot and Wet, and Cold and Dry) instead of the twelve months, and these were indicated by pictures (see Figure 4). The Korail *bustee* boys plotted the same trends on the chart with the exception of 'Food Expenditure' ('General Expenditure' remained), and with the addition of a 'Helping Parents' category. These were also represented entirely by pictures for the Korail group (see Figure 4).

The trends indicated on the seasonal charts represent the combined opinions of two groups of waste pickers. They can be used to 'cross check' the findings of individual discussions as well as discussion with dealers. In addition, trends within the chart can be used to justify or validate other trends within the chart itself. Asking the participants about the links between different trends will often reveal whether they have filled in the chart consistently, for example, with regard a relationship between climate and ill health. In addition, the chart can

Figure 4. Pictures used in the Korail seasonal chart

Expenditure

  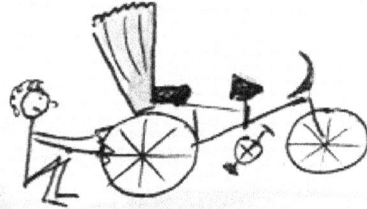

Helping parents

  **'Cold and dry'**

 **'Hot and Dry'**  **'Hot and Wet'**

Sketches: Jonathan Rouse

be used to clarify questions which otherwise appear to be very similar, such as 'Waste available' and 'Waste income'.

3.2.3 Ranking exercise

The children carried out a simple ranking exercise in which they were given a set of picture cards indicating different aspects of their lives, such as family, security, food, money, friends, clothes etc. Before the exercise began, each card was held up in turn and the participants were asked to describe what they thought the pictures represented. Of the 14 cards, only the card depicting freedom was misunderstood; this was a concept not easily represented in a drawing. After ensuring that they understood the meaning of these cards they were asked to rank them in order of their perceived importance.

For the first group in Mirpur, it was felt that the card depicting 'money' was too vague, and that it should be possible to draw a distinction between having *enough money* (i.e. meeting basic needs), and having *lots of money* (i.e. being rich). For the ranking exercise with the second group in the Korail *bustee*, two such cards were used. The cards were ranked second and third most important respectively by the Korail group but after some questioning it was felt that the participants had not understood the difference. Simplicity is clearly important.

Figure 5 shows the cards depicting 'Good friends', 'Family' and 'Good clothes' used in the ranking exercise.

3.3 Recognising different backgrounds and perspectives

This section explores some issues resulting from the fact that participants are from very different backgrounds from those of the field workers undertaking this research. While the researchers are educated and literate, the pickers have had little or no formal education, and are mostly illiterate. In addition, in this research, the primary field worker and participants are from different countries, continents and cultures and speak different languages. These differences each pose their own problems which need to be overcome with considerable thought and care.

In the course of discussions with pickers, it appeared that sometimes they were being asked about concepts they had never before considered or analysed. Others appeared to have difficulty understanding the questions being asked or thinking about certain concepts. Many such examples related to questions about trends and seasonality.

Some of the issues and concepts tackled within the SLA are complex. Concepts familiar to the facilitator may seem obscure to the participant and prove impossible to grasp. The consideration of some aspects involves skills such as hypothesising, which may be alien (and seem quite superfluous) to a picker. The reasons for this communication difficulty could be that the pickers simply do not have the mental capacity or skills to consider such 'complex'

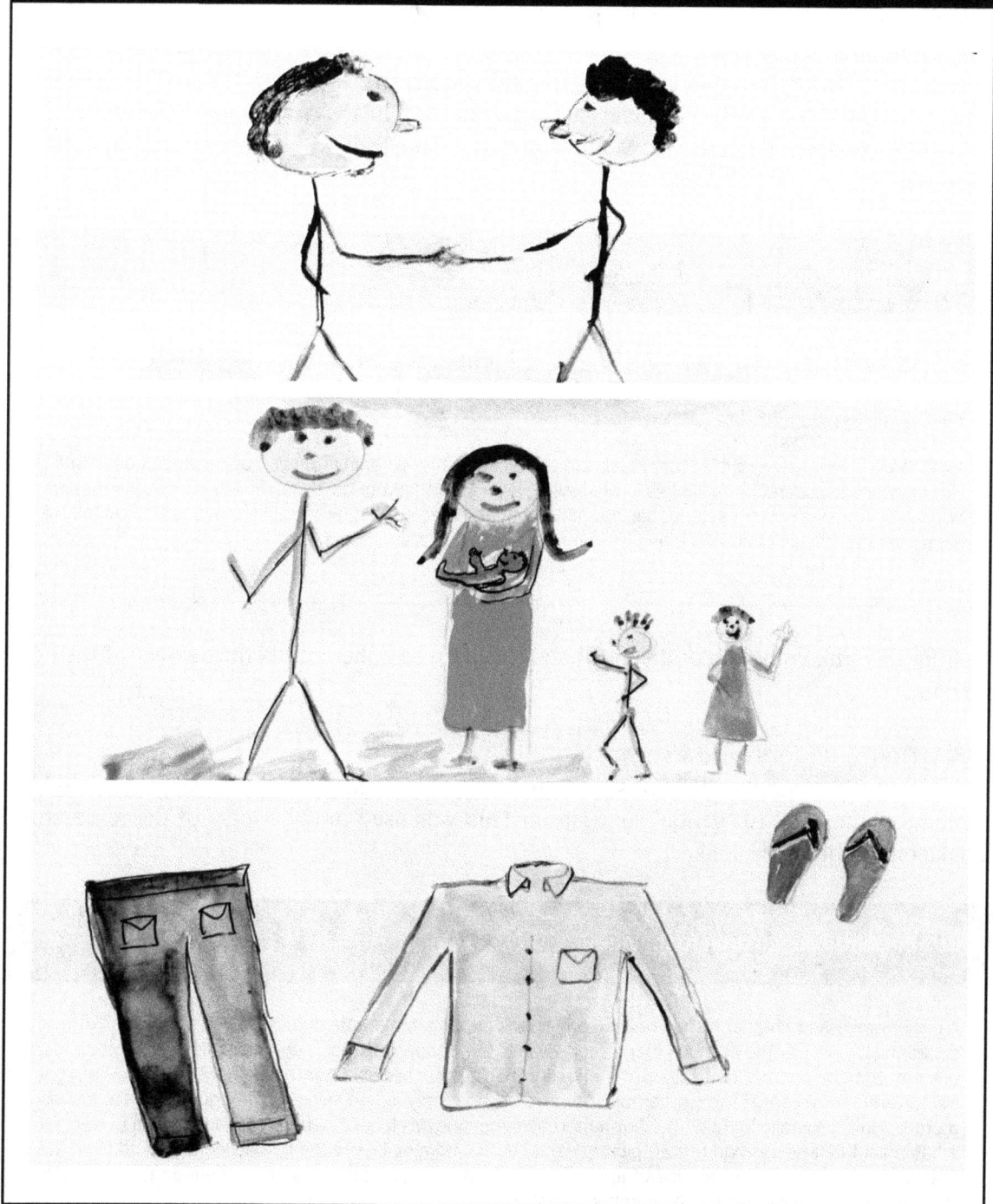

Figure 5: Cards used in the ranking exercise

Sketches: Jonathan Rouse. The results of the ranking exercise are presented in Section 6.1 of Part I.

issues. This is genuinely unlikely however, and the findings in Dhaka strongly suggested that this was not the case. A more likely explanation for communication problems is that the pickers can, and do, think about the issues, but in a *different way* from the facilitator. The distinction between *'not thinking'* and *'thinking in a different way'* is an important issue to understand. The key to unlocking people's knowledge may be in understanding *how* they think, and *why*. Practically, this means asking a question in a way relevant to the picker. The following example illustrates how not doing this can lead to confusion and misleading responses.

Box 7. Understanding the question: making links

A waste picker is aware that the number of other pickers has increased in a particular area over the last few years. He has reacted by arriving at that place progressively earlier in the morning and finding new areas in which to pick later in the day.

A researcher asks him about trends, which are explained to him as 'things which have changed over time'. Having never considered the changes in his picking area in this light or as 'dynamic processes', he answers no. In fact – he has noticed a trend, has thought about and reacted to it, but he just saw it as a 'change'. He does not make the link between it and what the researcher is asking about.

Making this link is the job of a careful and skilled researcher and is the subject of the next section.

3.3.1 Being understood by participants

The following example illustrates one such way of forging the link using the (slightly contentious) method of 'gentle' suggestion. This was used in the course of the research in Dhaka on various occasions.

Box 8. Gentle suggestion technique

A picker was asked whether he had noticed any trends relating to his work during the last few years. Without appearing to consider the question much, he answered no. Suspecting that there were perhaps some trends, but that the boy had not understood the question, the researcher said 'We have spoken to some of your friends and they said that the city corporation have begun emptying the skips more frequently in the last six months. Have you noticed that?' The boy remembers that this has indeed happened, and goes on to say that it has meant that he has had to start picking earlier in the morning before the first collection. In addition, he now understands exactly what type of information is being sought, and goes on to mention further trends including an overall increase in the number of pickers.

This method should only be used when open-ended enquiry has elicited no response. Care is required, and its use should be recorded in field notes. In the research for this study it was found to be a useful way of deciding if there were actually no trends or if the participant simply could not think of any or had not understood the question. This technique is one step away from the ideal of no suggestion at all, but is a long way from the worst-case scenario of asking a loaded question at the outset.

It is essential to find ways of making concepts accessible to pickers and of 'unlocking' their views and knowledge. A further important aspect of this process is enabling people to express themselves in a way in which they feel comfortable. This is likely to be different from the technical form of expression usually employed by the researcher, and is further discussed in the next section.

3.4 Invisible trends

The presence of trends was investigated with waste pickers to help develop an understanding of how aspects of their livelihoods have changed over time, and how they are likely to change in the future. These were generally investigated in discussions with individual pickers, and involved them identifying changes they had noticed in any aspect of their livelihood since beginning picking. Pickers mentioned a small number of trends mostly relating to the composition and quantity of waste. These had directly impacted their work and their effects had been clearly visible to them.

It is possible that other trends existed but were not mentioned. One reason for this may be that trends, pertinent to the lives and livelihoods of pickers, were combining in such a way that their effects were negated. Such trends would thus not be noticed by pickers and would remain unmentioned. This illustrates the possibility that important trends exist but remain overlooked in research. The following fictitious examples further illustrate how this might happen.

Box 9. Invisible trends

1. The quantity of valuable waste on the streets may have declined significantly over a period of time, but with it the number of pickers also declined, so the net effects on the livelihoods of remaining pickers was zero.

2. The quantity of waste on the streets may have increased over time, but a picker already picked as much as he or she could carry before this, so the increase made no difference to income.

A similar problem was highlighted in the seasonality discussions, illustrated overleaf

---

Box 9. Invisible trends *continued*

3. Raju reports that his income remains steady throughout the year. It was therefore assumed that quantities and prices of waste also remained steady throughout the year. However, in the course of further discussion, it transpires that during the wet season the value of waste decreases but he is able to collect more in the ponds near his home. Hence, the overall effect on income is zero.

In these examples, trends or seasonal variations exist but their effects are not apparent in the livelihoods of the pickers. In other circumstances, a single trend may be reported which appears straightforward but which is in fact the complex product of two or more different trends combined. The following demonstrates how this may happen.

Box 9. Invisible trends *continued*

4. The value of waste may have declined over a period, but in that time a given picker grew older and stronger and was able to pick, carry and sell significantly more waste. Therefore, despite the decline in value of waste the picker enjoyed a rise in income.

These hypothetical examples demonstrate the need for great care and thoroughness in research and data collection. They also highlight the need for cross-checking techniques such as triangulation, described in Section 4.5. A consideration of 'invisible' trends may be vital to the planning of effective interventions.

3.5 Ambiguity

In addition to the problems of overlooking or misinterpreting trends, there is also the danger that questions be misinterpreted through ambiguity. On occasions, different pickers can also describe a situation in different ways according to their perspective or the way in which they have understood the question. One such example occurred in the course of the Dhaka research, and related to questions about the 'amount of waste available' during different seasons. The ambiguity of this question was not realised until some way into the research. The pickers' answers could reflect either the quantity of valuable waste *available for picking* or the quantity actually *collected and sold*. These may be very different. The fictitious example below, based on real experience in the course of the research, demonstrates how this ambiguity can be problematic.

Box 10. An illustration of the pitfalls of ambiguity

In a given area the quantity of waste available for picking remains constant throughout all seasons. During the wet season many pickers choose to collect and sell less waste because the work is unpleasant, and as a result, their incomes from waste picking decrease. Because there are fewer pickers on the streets, those who continue picking during the wet season have access to a greater proportion of the valuable waste (less competition), so their incomes *increase*.

In answer to the question 'How does the amount of waste change during the year?' three equally correct answers could be given depending on the perspective of the picker and the way in which they understood the question. 'It decreases' according to the pickers who work less during the wet season and are referring to how much they collect and sell. 'It remains constant' for those pickers referring to the amount of waste on the street irrespective of their picking habits. 'It increases' from the perspective of the pickers who continue picking and are referring to the amount of waste available to them.

It is difficult to be sure of the degree to which this ambiguity was an issue for this research, in part because all answers were translated. However, it is another important demonstration of the need for care and clarity in questioning techniques.

Photograph 9. Waste pickers in the Korail *bustee*

4.
Other issues

4.1 Fear of authority and attitudes to field staff

One aspect of understanding participants is trying to understand how they perceive the field workers themselves. On first visits to areas or upon first meetings, participants would often look scared, submissive and be very closed and quiet. Some feared the fieldworkers might be from the municipal authorities or the police, and in the slum areas there was reportedly concern that they were government representatives, perhaps assessing land for its development potential. A fear of 'authorities' amongst pickers is in many ways justified for a number of reasons, some of which are described in Part I. In one *bustee* the author was mistaken for a tourist and the translator was accused of taking money for 'showing off' the poor of Dhaka. This was another reason not for fear of, but general negative attitudes towards, fieldworkers.

These examples highlight the importance of forging trusting relationships with participants. In the time scale of this research this was possible with only a few of the boys. These were in the Korail *bustee* which was visited on at least five occasions, and the Mirpur Hostel which was visited by one or other of the researchers three times. Knowing, and being known, by some of the inhabitants by name, and having gained general familiarity undoubtedly did much for improving the ease with which views, opinions and experiences could be exchanged.

4.2 Crowds and attention

The effects of crowds, onlookers and attention were undoubtedly the single most disruptive factor experienced in the field work. In most research areas in Dhaka when the fieldworkers paused, a crowd would gather interested in knowing what was happening. This was a particular problem in the poorer areas of town where researchers, let alone white researchers, are not a common site. It would be likely to be less of a problem if the researchers were all Bangladeshi.

For some participants the attention was welcome, but for most (particularly older boys) it was not. It seemed remaining inconspicuous was important. In one instance, crowds caused a picker (Jushim in Begum Bari) to terminate the interview because he said he was too 'embarrassed'.

In the case of the focus groups it was difficult to prevent other children and adults gathered around from adding their own opinions or 'helping' the children think through the concepts presented to them. In these circumstances, due to our indebtedness to the hostel owner or the school teacher who had enabled the groups to take place, it was difficult to politely ask them not to participate.

The problem with crowds on the streets was overcome to a great extent by discussing issues 'on the move'. Keeping moving shed the curious children, and also meant that the participant would spend more time working. It was often useful to stop to discuss some of the more complex issues, such as seasonality, with pickers. For this a place was generally chosen away from where they lived, often in a roadside tea shop.

4.3 Time

Time exercised a constraint on the thoroughness of research with individual participants, and it was important to accept that it would not be possible (or reasonable) to try to elicit information for a comprehensive livelihood profile from a single interviewee. The time required to do this would result in loss of income for the picker, and may lead to loss of concentration for interviewer and interviewee alike. Concentration was a problem during some of the interviews as pickers wished to return to their work, and some clearly (and perhaps understandably) had little interest in the issues being discussed.

It is important to be sensitive towards the feelings and wishes of participants, particularly when they are giving their time freely for something from which they may never benefit. The Dhaka research highlighted the importance of being well prepared and organised in order to optimise the time spent with pickers. It was also important to know when to stop; younger pickers lost patience, others felt embarrassed or scared and others just wanted to return to their work.

4.4 Motivation behind answers

This report is based on the assumption that pickers tell the truth in the answers they give. However, it is important to accept that pickers may be providing spurious information for a variety of reasons. Three such reasons may be that:

- participants are trying to give you the answers they assume you wish to hear. This may be exaggerated in cases where participants feel threatened or intimidated by the researcher;

- participants base their answers on the assumption that they will determine the nature or extent of future help. As such, they answer in the way they think they would be most likely to benefit; or,

- participants have been asked the same questions by many different researchers but have never benefited from any of the promised interventions. Given this, they provide spurious information because they feel angry, or simply for their own amusement (Tripathi, 2000).

These problems can each be combated by clarifying the purpose of the research, being honest about the benefits it will or *will not* bring them and by forging trusting relationships with participants. Other than that, it is important to be aware that this may be happening and to include in fieldwork ways of checking findings. One such way, 'triangulation', is described in the following section.

4.5 Cross-checking and triangulation

There were various occasions on which it was possible to cross-check information supplied by one picker with information from another, or from someone closely linked with pickers' work. It was useful to speak to a number of pickers in a given area in order to try to verify the accuracy of information given. It is of course quite possible that different answers can all be correct given that the circumstances of no two pickers are identical, but when findings from two similar pickers in a given area were different it was worthwhile investigating. Checking would either reveal genuine differences between pickers, or highlight misunderstandings on the part of the interviewee, researcher or even translator.

In addition to speaking to other pickers, another useful way to cross-check data was to speak to the dealers to whom the pickers sell their waste. Dealers are only concerned with how much waste is collected and sold to them, and not with the overall quantity of waste on the streets, or difficulties associated with its collection etc. A number of dealers were consulted in Dhaka and their statements often concurred with what pickers had said. Here are two examples.

Box 11. Triangulation: dealers' statements

At the Matuail dump, a dealer called Riyadge described how around 10% of the pickers stopped work altogether during the wet season, but that his business could actually improve during the rains because those that remain actually collected more waste. Riyadge concurs with Jussna's statement that when she continues picking during the wet season she finds valuable waste more easily.

Abdul Jumna, a dealer in the Begum Bari area who buys waste from participants Raju and Jushim said that overall business is better during the wet season. He stated that although the value of waste falls during the wet season the quantity increases sufficiently to mean that he is better off. This is consistent with Raju's description of the seasonal trends in waste.

Clearly, referring to people who interact with pickers and who have a stake and interest in their livelihoods is a valuable exercise and one that can serve to raise questions about, or confirm, the information gathered from pickers.

Even after triangulation, it is possible that the findings from each participant will disagree. An example of discrepancies between data collected from three different sources each referring to the Korail *bustee* area is described below.

Box 12. Discrepancies

In an individual discussion with Nasir of the Korail *bustee* he stated that he found more waste in the wet season. However, the question of seasonal waste trends in the Korail Focus Group (in which he was participating) was met with an emphatic answer of 'definitely less waste in the wet season'. Despite this, the dealer in Banani (to whom some of the group members sell waste) said there was very little difference in quantities of waste during the year.

This shows that, for some reason, either each of the parties experiences the effects of the seasons *in a given area* differently, or that two of the parties are misunderstanding the question and / or providing incorrect information. It raises the need for more investigation.

Photograph 10. Jussna and friends, pickers at the Matuail landfill site

4.6 Generalisation

In the course of research it became clear that it was not possible to treat or consider waste pickers as an homogeneous group. There were numerous variations in terms of their personalities, personal circumstances and the nature of their work. While most pickers had received no education, some had received a little. Some pickers were the main breadwinners in the family while others were just working to supplement household incomes, both factors that impacted their decision-making processes. Although most pickers were young boys, there were pickers of all ages and both sexes in Dhaka. In addition, pickers in different areas of Dhaka had access to different forms of waste and were even affected differently by the seasons.

It would be unwise to attempt to treat pickers as a single consistent group behaving in the same way and involved in a uniform occupation. A large sample would be required both to understand the composition of the waste-picking group in Dhaka, as well as to develop accurate and meaningful understanding of their livelihoods.

5.
Summary of findings

Part II of this booklet has described a number of the pitfalls encountered and lessons learned during the research in Dhaka. The main findings are outlined below.

- Choice of participant in research requires thought and care, and it is important to avoid listening only to the confident and loud and ignoring those with 'quiet voices'. It is important to be sure that data is collected from a variety of stakeholders.

- There are problems associated with the sex and nationality of researchers. These related to crowd attraction in the *bustees* resulting from the nationality (and appearance) of the main fieldworker, the problems presented by the need for a translator and the difficulties of male researchers working with female pickers.

- Unexpected results can arise and certain trends and effects can be 'hidden' and easily elude a researcher. This was the case with regards 'invisible trends' where apparently straightforward trends could actually be the result of two or more trends interacting.

- A general awareness of how questions are being interpreted, and recognising ambiguity is essential in fieldwork. Ambiguity arose through language and translation problems as well as through more fundamental misunderstandings due to differences in perspective. The careful use of 'gentle suggestion' and ways of aiding pickers' understanding of issues, concepts and questions can also be valuable.

- Incorporation of cross checking and 'triangulation' techniques into the research is important. It is vital to appreciate that discrepancies in data may be because of inaccuracies, misunderstandings or genuine differences between participants.

- Research with groups and individuals are both valuable and likely to provide different types of information. The ability of young, uneducated and illiterate pickers to express themselves vocally, as well as through group exercises such as seasonal charting and ranking, should not be underestimated. It is important however to recognise, understand, and respond to differences in the abilities of pickers to communicate.

■ Pickers' attitudes towards field staff need to be understood. Taking time to develop relationships and understand participants can encourage and enable more open and honest discussion.

■ The motivation behind answers may not always be obvious or simple and it is important to interpret responses accordingly.

The box below summarises the kinds of questions a researcher should be asking to keep in mind the pitfalls and lessons learned from this research.

Box 13. Field worker questions

■ What other explanations are there for findings? Ambiguity, interplay of different factors, combinations of trends etc.?

■ On what grounds am I choosing my participants in this research? How relevant is this participant to the purpose of this research? Am I giving everyone a fair hearing?

■ Am I giving this picker the opportunity to express himself in a way in which he feels comfortable?

■ Am I being understood? Are the questions ambiguous? Am I asking them about things in a way relevant to them, or me? How are communication problems mani festing themselves and who are these problems between (myself / translator / picker)?

■ Do communication difficulties run deeper than the language alone (i.e. fundamentally different perspectives)?

■ How can I cross-check and verify the information I am getting?

■ Am I being reasonable to this picker? Am I disrupting his work or embarrassing him? Am I outstaying my welcome?

References

The Department for International Development (DFID) (1999) *Sustainable Livelihoods Guidance Sheets.* DFID: London UK.

Folch-Lyon, E. and Trost, J.F. (1981) Conducting Focus Group Sessions. *Studies in Family Planning.* Vol 12, No 12.

Search, H. (2000) (DFID consultant working with garment workers in Dhaka) Personal communication (Meeting).

Tripathi, K.C. (2000) (Project Manager India Development Group UK (IDG UK) Lucknow, Uttar Pradesh, India) Personal communication (Discussion).

Bibliography

Ali, M. (1997) *Integration of informal and official systems in solid waste management.* PhD Thesis, Loughborough University.

Beall, J.B. (1999) *Recognising Livelihoods from Urban Waste. Synthesis note No. 4.* Water, Engineering and Development Centre: Loughborough University, UK.

Carney, D. (Ed.) (1998) *Sustainable Rural Livelihoods. What contribution can we make?* Department for International Development: London, UK.

Chambers, R. (1983) *Rural Development, Putting the Last First.* Longman: London.

Department for International Development (DFID) (1999) *Sustainable Livelihoods Guidance Sheets.* DFID: London, UK.

Freudy, C. and Alamgir, A. (1992) Case Study 1: Street Pickers in Calcutta Slums. *Environment and Urbanization* Vol 4, No 2.

Grandstaff, W.S. and Grandstaff, T.B. (circa 1998) *Semi-Structured Interviewing by Multidisciplinary Teams in RRA.* Publisher unknown. Located in the Institute of Development Studies participation reading room, Sussex, UK.

Johnson, V; Ivan-Smith, E; Gordon, G; Pridmore, P. and Scott, P. (1998) *Stepping Forward. Children and Young People's participation in the development process*. Intermediate Technology Publications Ltd: London.

Kazi, Noor M. (1999) *Citizens Guide for Dhaka*. Environmental and Development Associates: Bangladesh.

Internet sources

Care International. (2000) Information on the CARE International Sustainable Livelihoods Approach. <http://www.care.org/> (February 2000)

Institute of Development Studies (2000) Information relating to participatory methodologies, including the guidance notes by Robert Chambers.<http://www.ids.ac.uk/ids/participt/index.html> (February 2000)

Department for International Development All DFID Sustainable Livelihoods information was obtained from this site. <http://www.livelihoods.org> (February 2000)

United Nations Development Programme Sustainable Livelihoods Unit. Various documents including general SL overviews, 'A guidebook for Field Projects: Participatory Research for Sustainable Livelihoods', 'Empowering people: a guide to participation' and 'Sustainable Livelihoods Concept Paper'. <http://www.undp.org/sl> (February 2000)

End notes

[1] It has been suggested that this fire was not entirely accidental, and that this is a method employed by the local authorities to make demolition of slums appear accidental.

[2] The possibility that the discrepancies are due to the way in which pickers have understood the questions is explored in 'Field Notes' Section 3.3.

[3] Source: DFID 'ESTEEM' primary education programme, Dhaka.

[4] This issue was discussed with Henrietta Search, a DFID consultant engaged in research in the garments industry in Dhaka. According to her, training periods generally last 2–3 weeks and trainees are required to have some existing sewing skills and, officially, be 14 years of age or older. The larger firms pay 50% salary during the training period, while many of the smaller firms pay nothing.

[5] The relationship between pickers and the police is described in more detail in Section 5 'Transforming Structures and Processes'.

[6] When walking through Banani with Saddam he pointed out the various trees in gardens from which he stole fruit. A number of other boys picked fruit from market floors and sold it on the streets.

[7] The Korail *Bustee* group said that during the wet season, one of the reasons they ate poorly was because of the shortage, and high price, of fuel for cooking.

[8] Another hostel run by the Swiss / Bangladesh NGO *Aparajeyo.*

Other solid waste management titles

Down to Earth
Mansoor Ali, Andrew Cotton and Ken Westlake

This book aims to help improve the poor practices of municipal solid waste management that prevail in many low-income countries.

Process of Change
Mansoor Ali and Andrew Cotton

These field notes present the findings of a focused research into the actual processes of change in low-income countries.

Success and Sustainability Indicators
A tool to assess primary collection schemes
Jenny Appleton, Mansoor Ali and Andrew Cotton

These indicators were prepared to help fieldworkers undertake impact assessments of primary solid waste collection schemes.
This bookl presents the indicators, how they may be used and the results of the field tests.

Synthesis notes on solid waste management
Series Editor: Mansoor Ali

These synthesis notes have been compiled to present an overview of current themes in solid waste management. The series includes six titles.

To order, please contact:
WEDC Publications
Loughborough University
LE11 3TU UK
Email: wedc@lboro.ac.uk

or order online from
www.lboro.ac.uk/wedc/publications

www.ingramcontent.com/pod-product-compliance
Lightning Source LLC
Chambersburg PA
CBHW080254030426
42334CB00023BA/2810